The Art of Adrian Velez

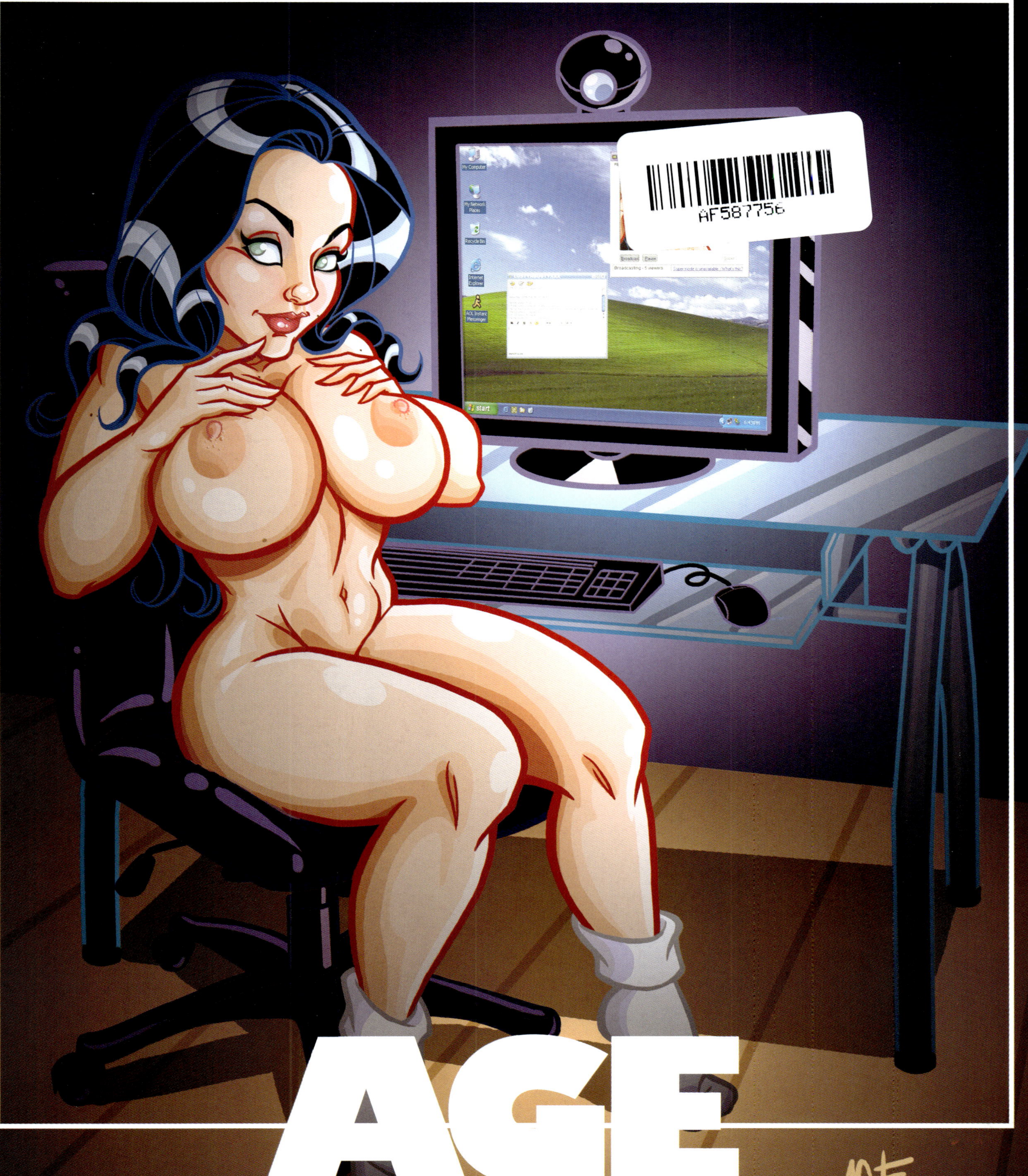

AGE
OF DELIGHTS!

AN SQP PRESENTATION

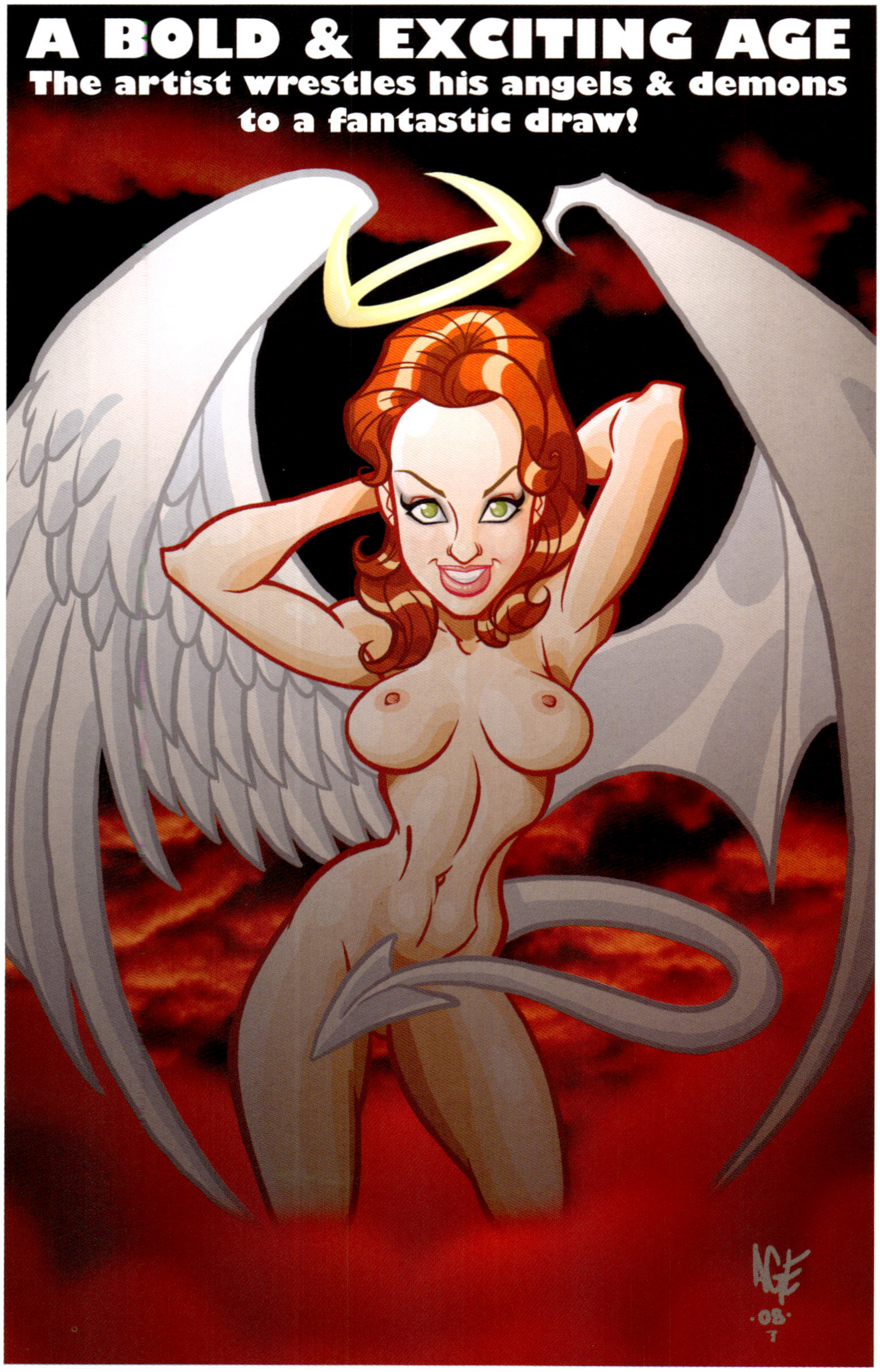

A BOLD & EXCITING AGE

The artist wrestles his angels & demons to a fantastic draw!

AGE ·08·

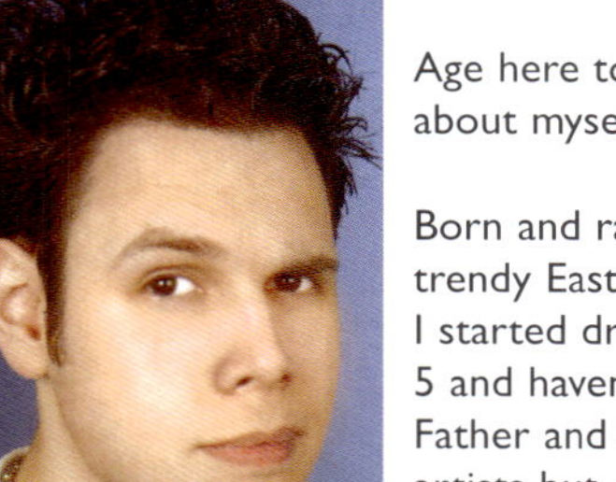

Hi!

Age here to tell you a little about myself.

Born and raised in New York's trendy East Village in 1976, I started drawing when I was 5 and haven't stopped since. Father and brothers were all artists but quit when they hit their teens, I continued to push forward because I heard there was profit to be made in this field. That, and girls always dig artists! Hehehe!

In my late teens I was introduced to the world of the comic convention. There I met some of the coolest and sexiest con girls who took a fancy to my art. Working with models like Manon Kelley, Avery Misuraca, Vera Vanguard, just to name a few. I also met many comic book artists, Louis Small Jr. in particular, took me under his wing and introduced to me other fine artists. He gave me some pointers on my art as well as how to pick up beautiful models.

After learning all I could from Louis I drifted into the world of photography. I got to work with the talented Robert Milazzo, and through him met several celebrities, models, and Playboy bunnies. I had a great time at Robert's studio, picking up techniques and working with so many models. It was great but ended too soon.

I then found myself working for tattoo artist Mario Barth, advertising his Las Vegas tattoo store at the Mandalay Bay Hotel. It was my biggest job to date and my illustrations were seen by many people. There was even a slot machine made which features my art, so check it out when you're there.

Now I'm working with my best bud and partner, Tom Chu and his company, Color Dojo on different projects.

All the art featured in this book were drawn by hand and then scanned into the computer to be colored. They are based on my dearest and closest models that stuck with me through the years. This book would not be possible if not for their beauty, love, and friendship.

Thank you girls, all of you are my angels.

Hope you enjoy the book!

Adrian (AGE) Velez

The Art of Adrian Velez
Age of Delights
Volume One

Book design by Grassy Knoll Studios.

Published by
SQP Inc.
PO Box 248 - Columbus, NJ 08022

Sal Quartuccio & Bob Keenan - Publishers

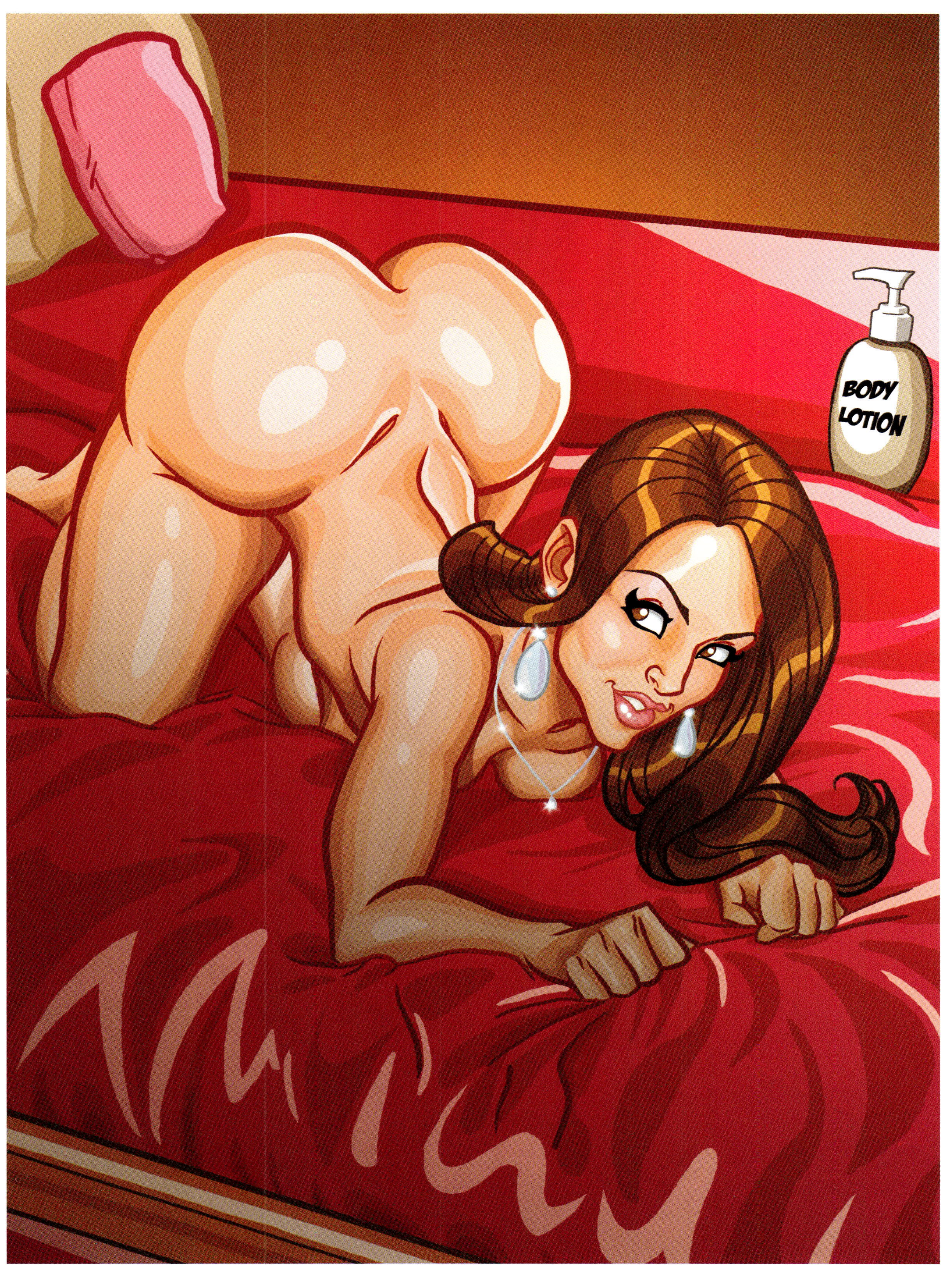
BODY
LOTION

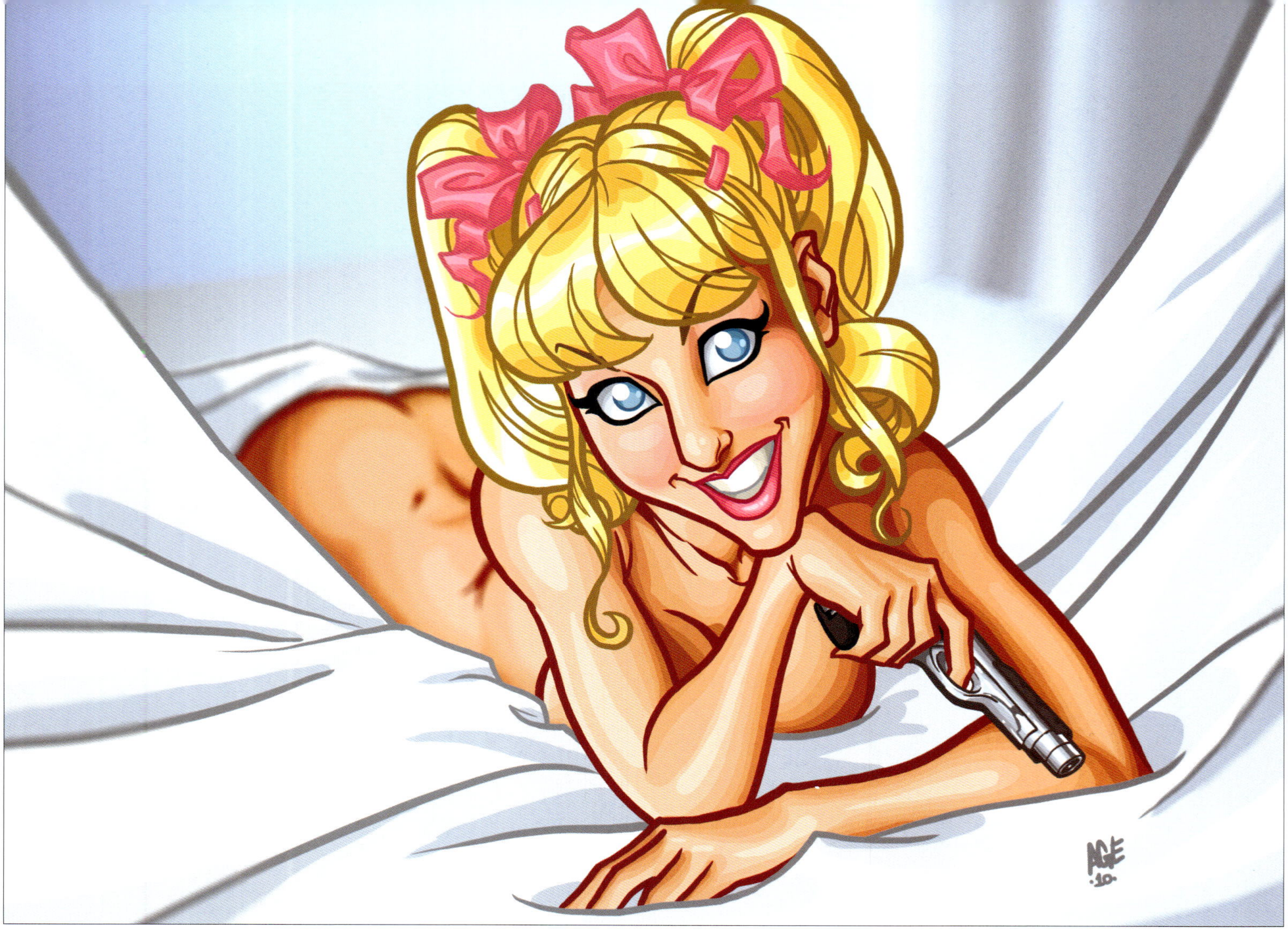

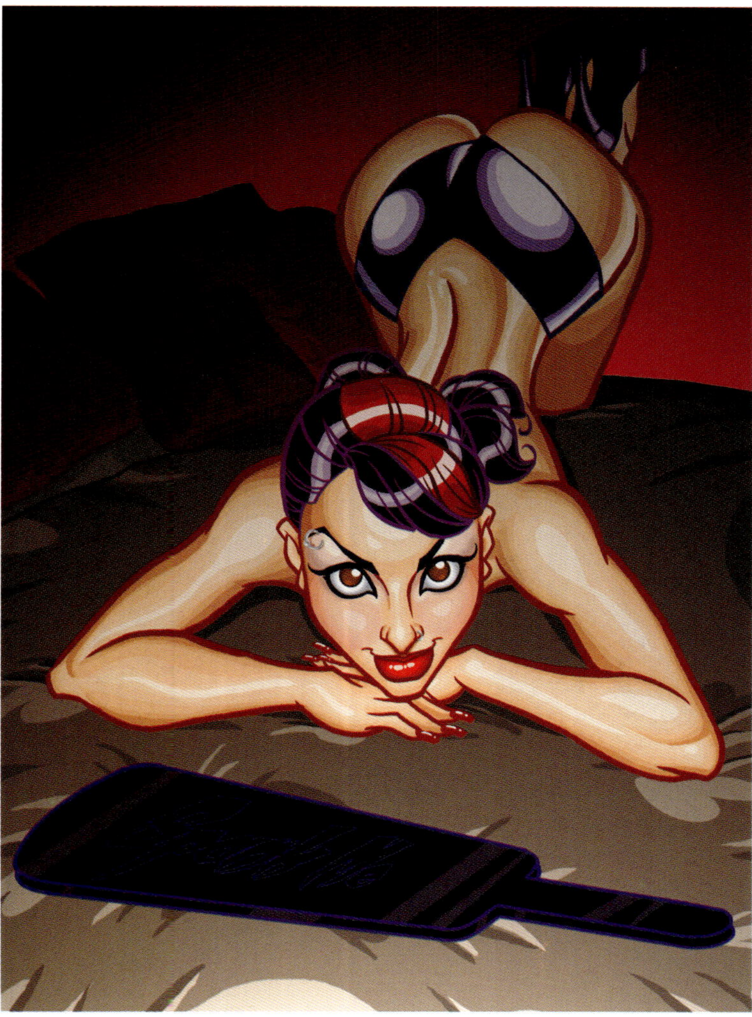

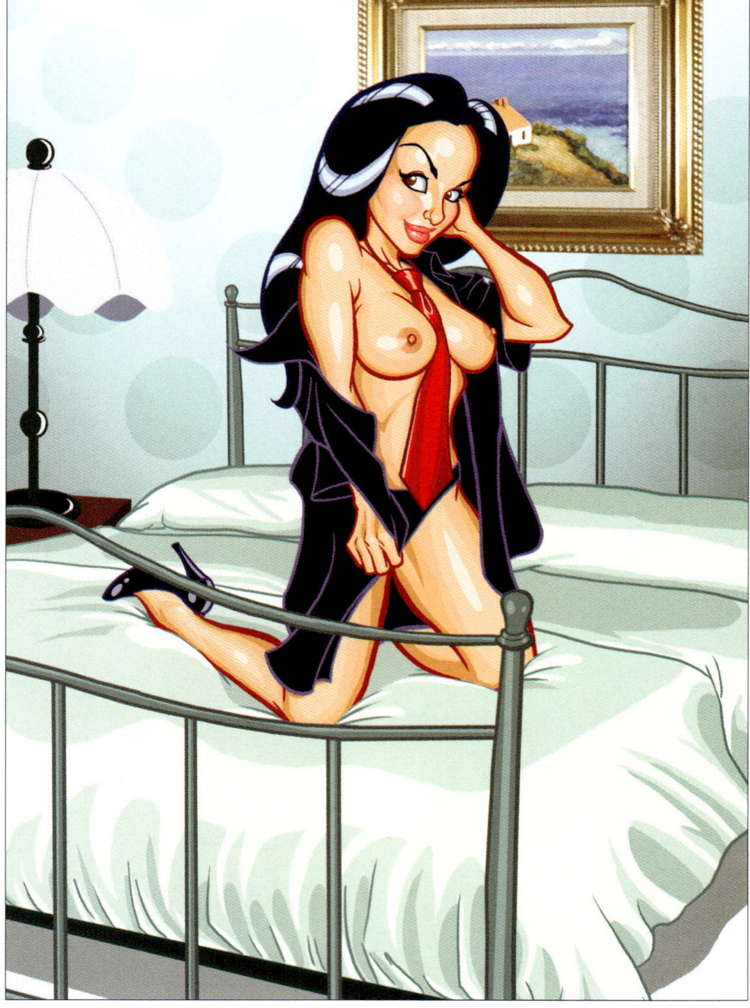

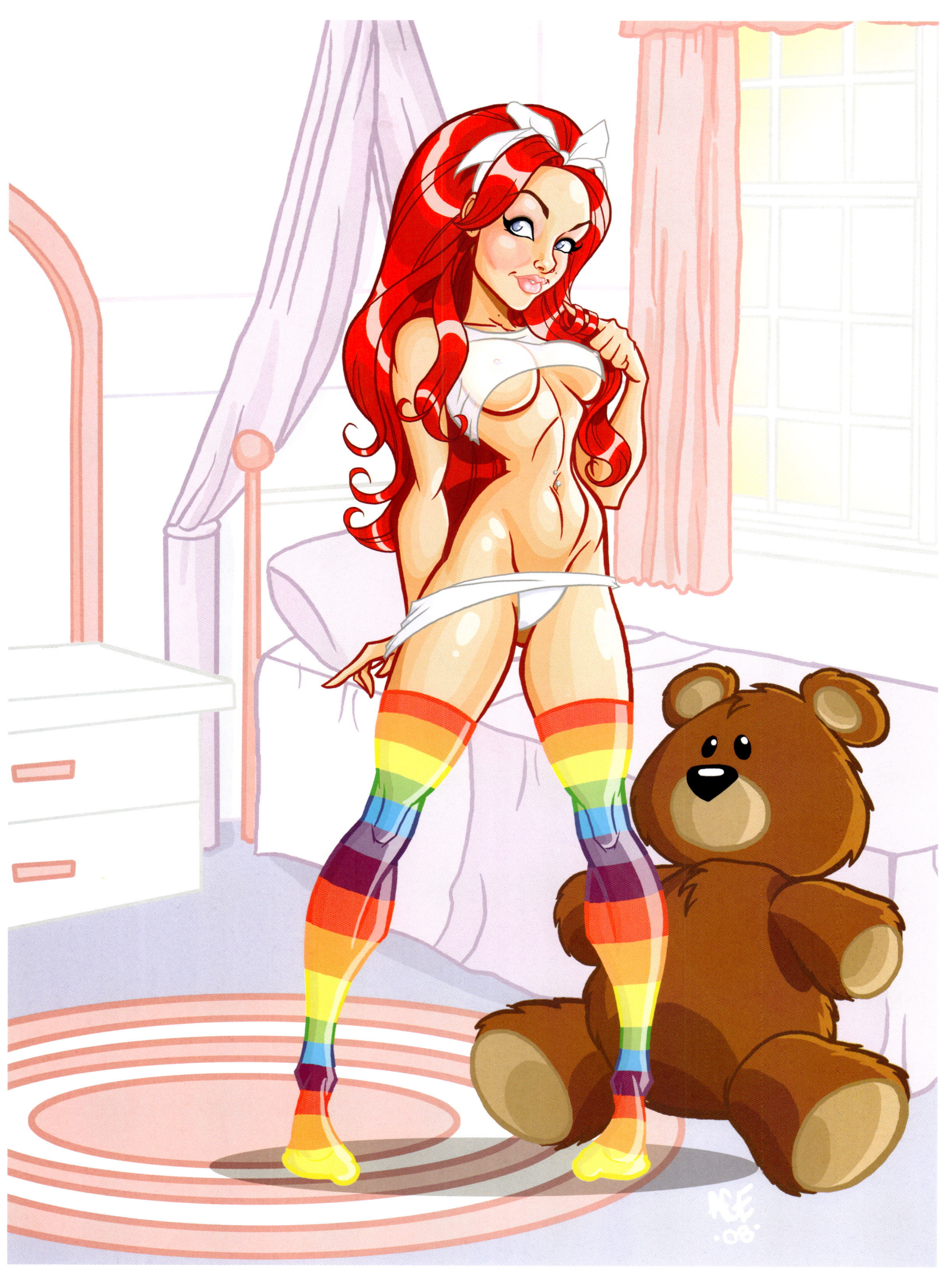

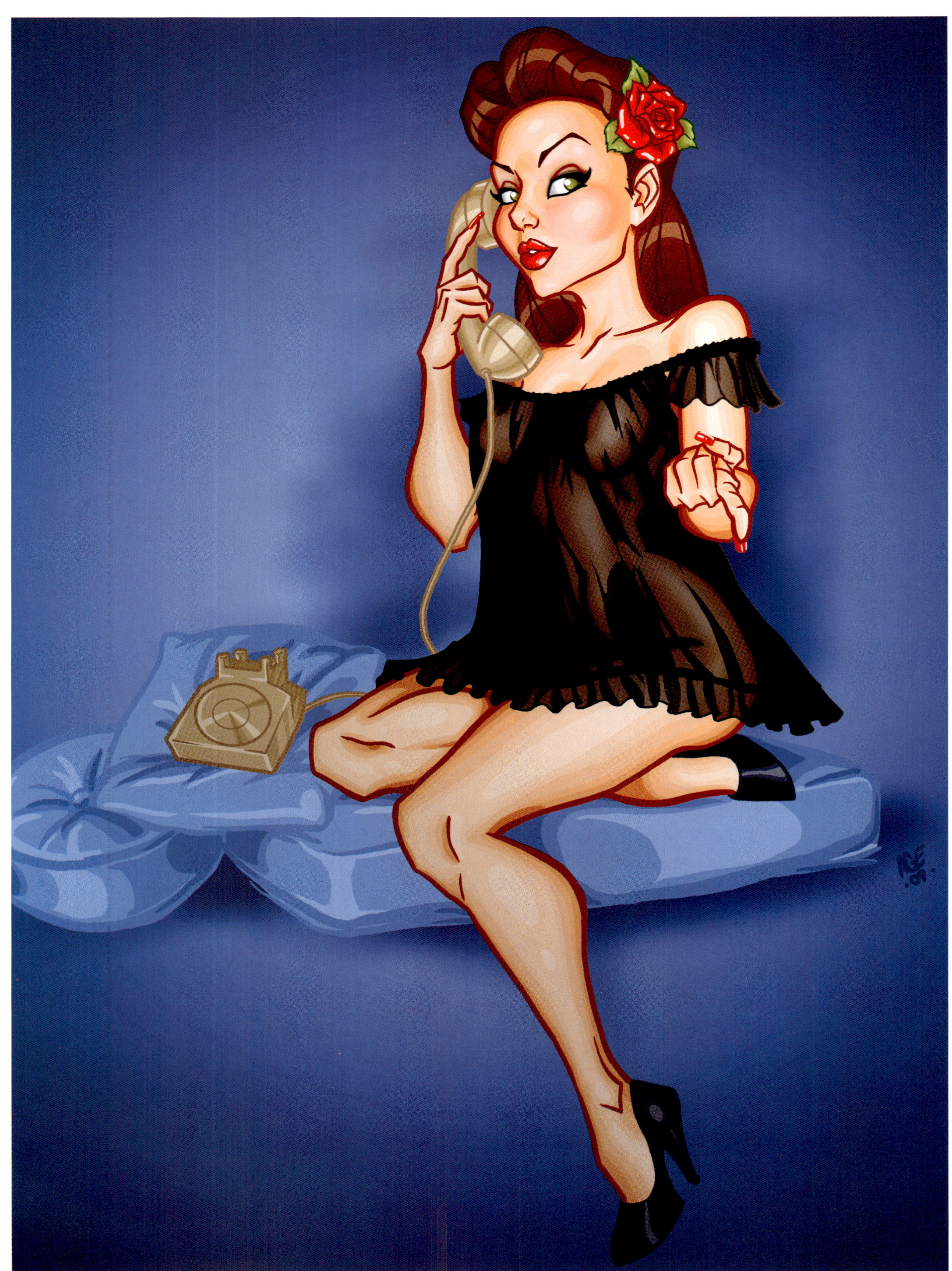

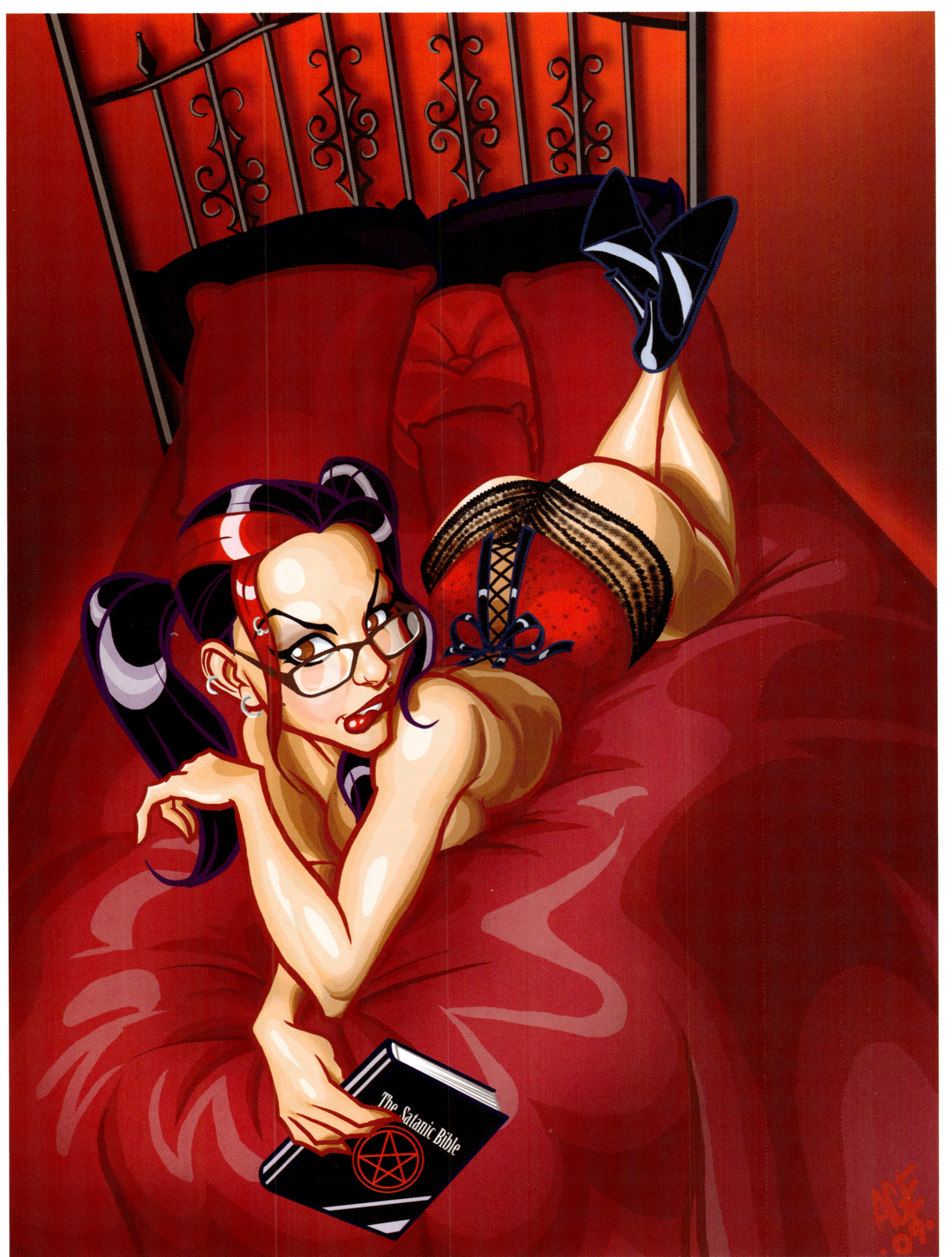
The Satanic Bible
AGE
.09.

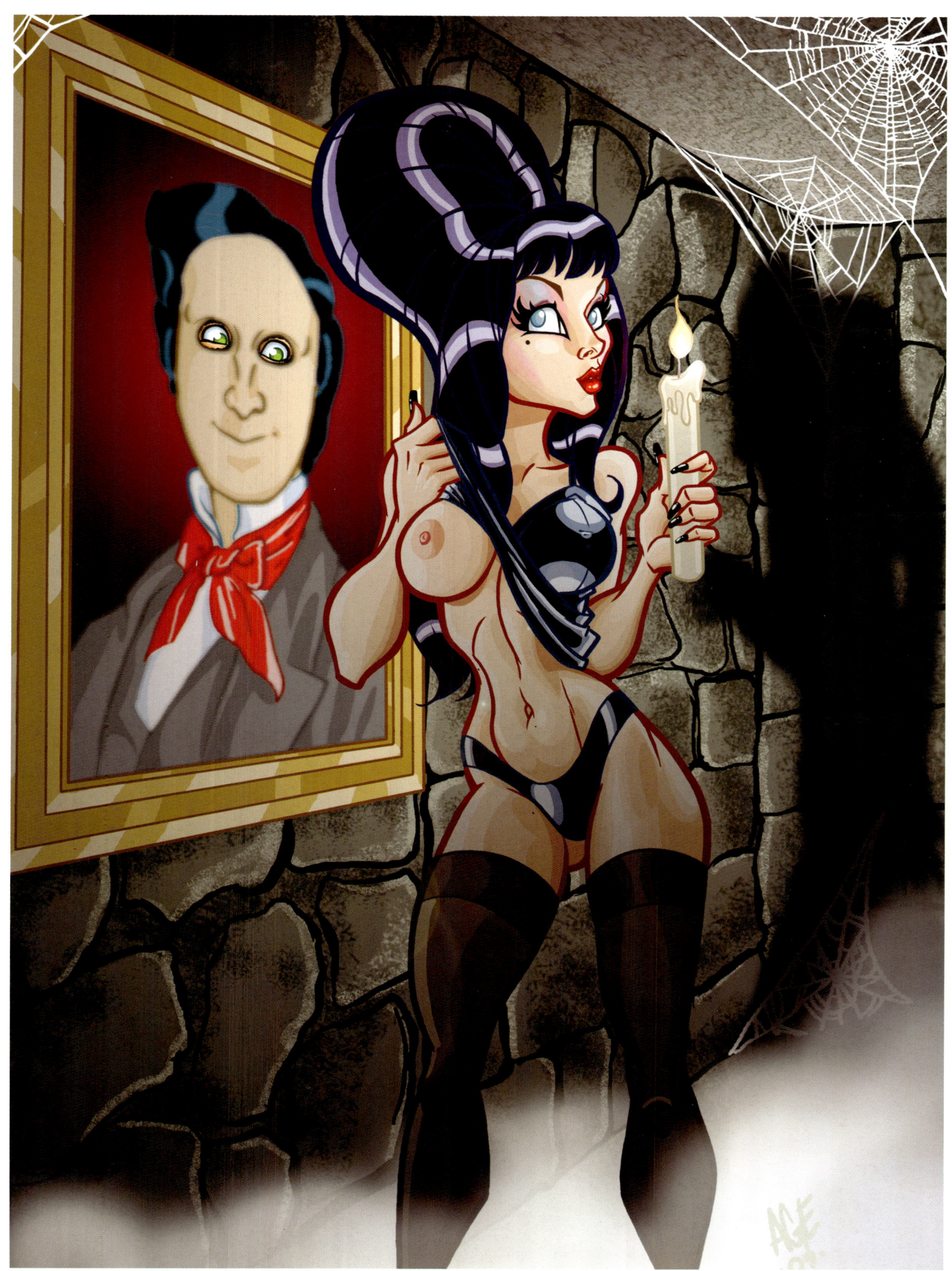

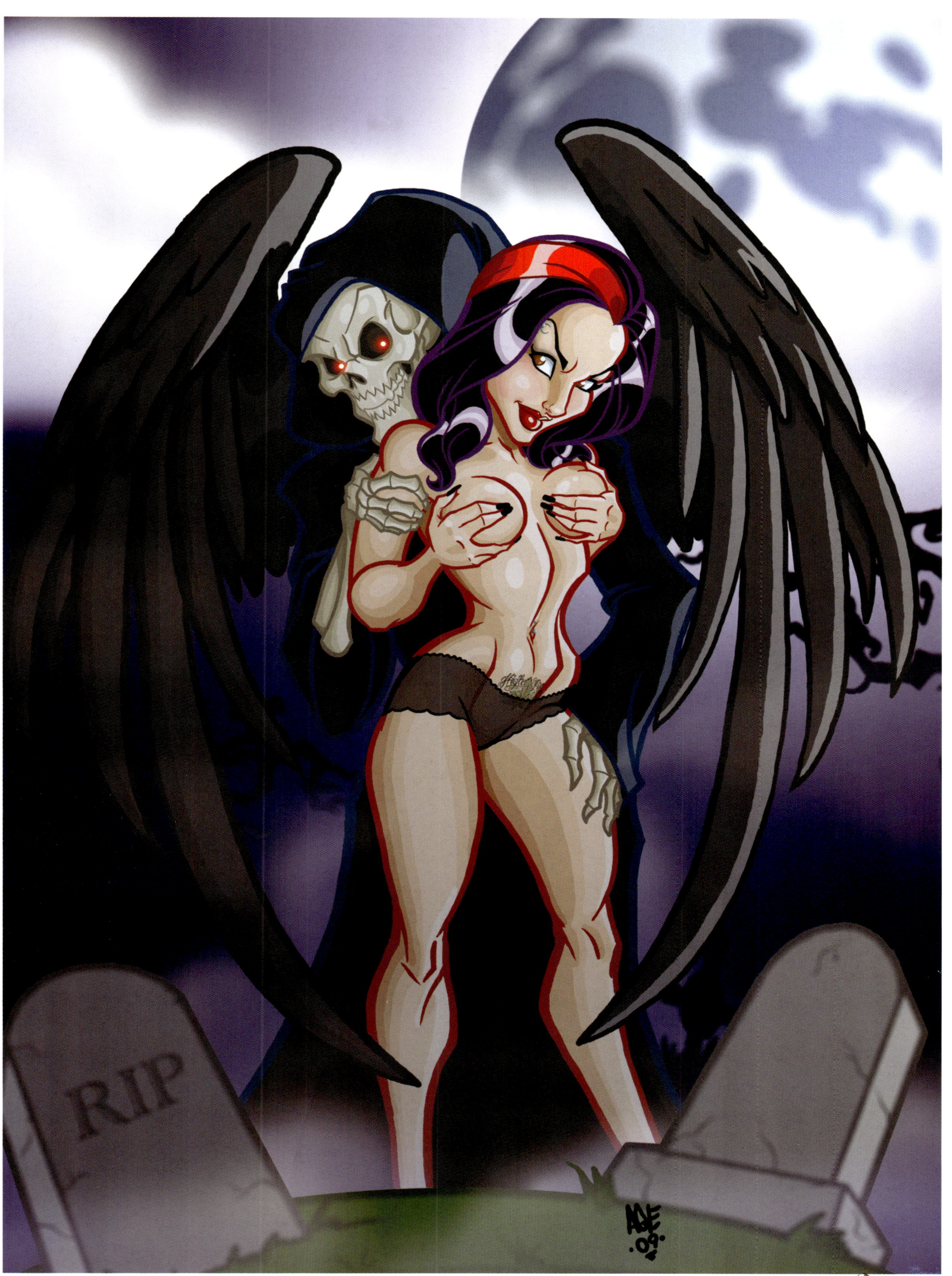
RIP
ADE
·09·

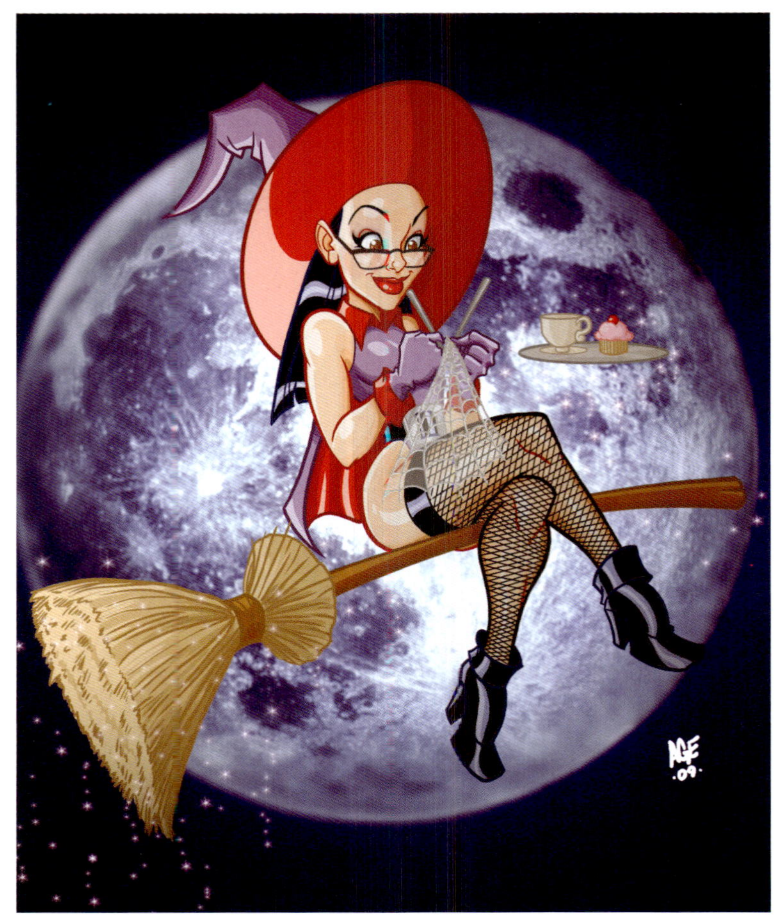

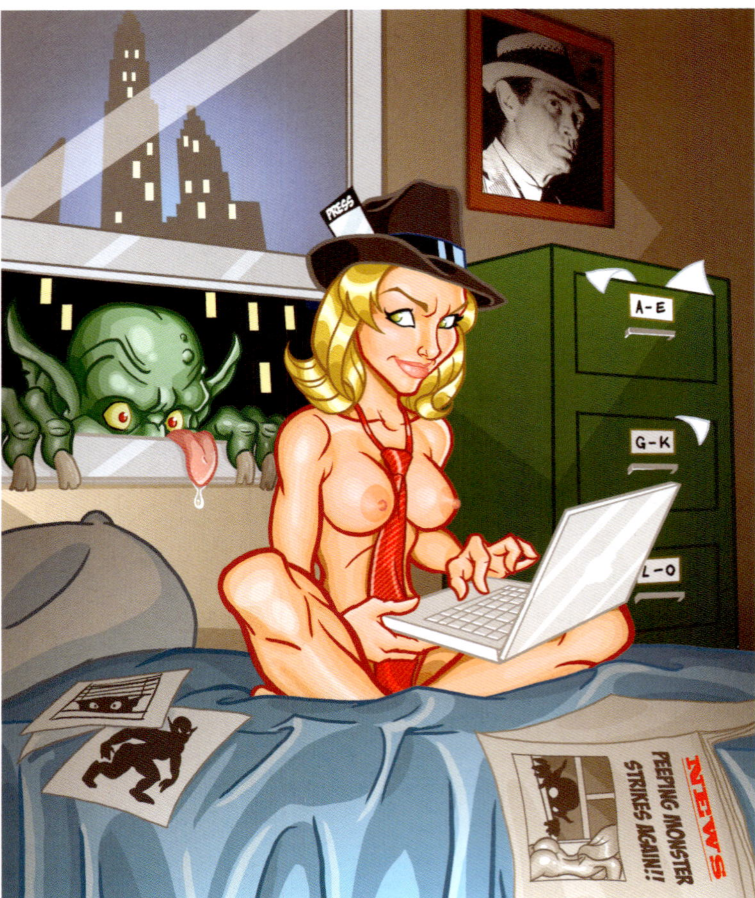
PRESS
A-E
G-K
L-O
NEWS
PEEPING MONSTER
STRIKES AGAIN!!

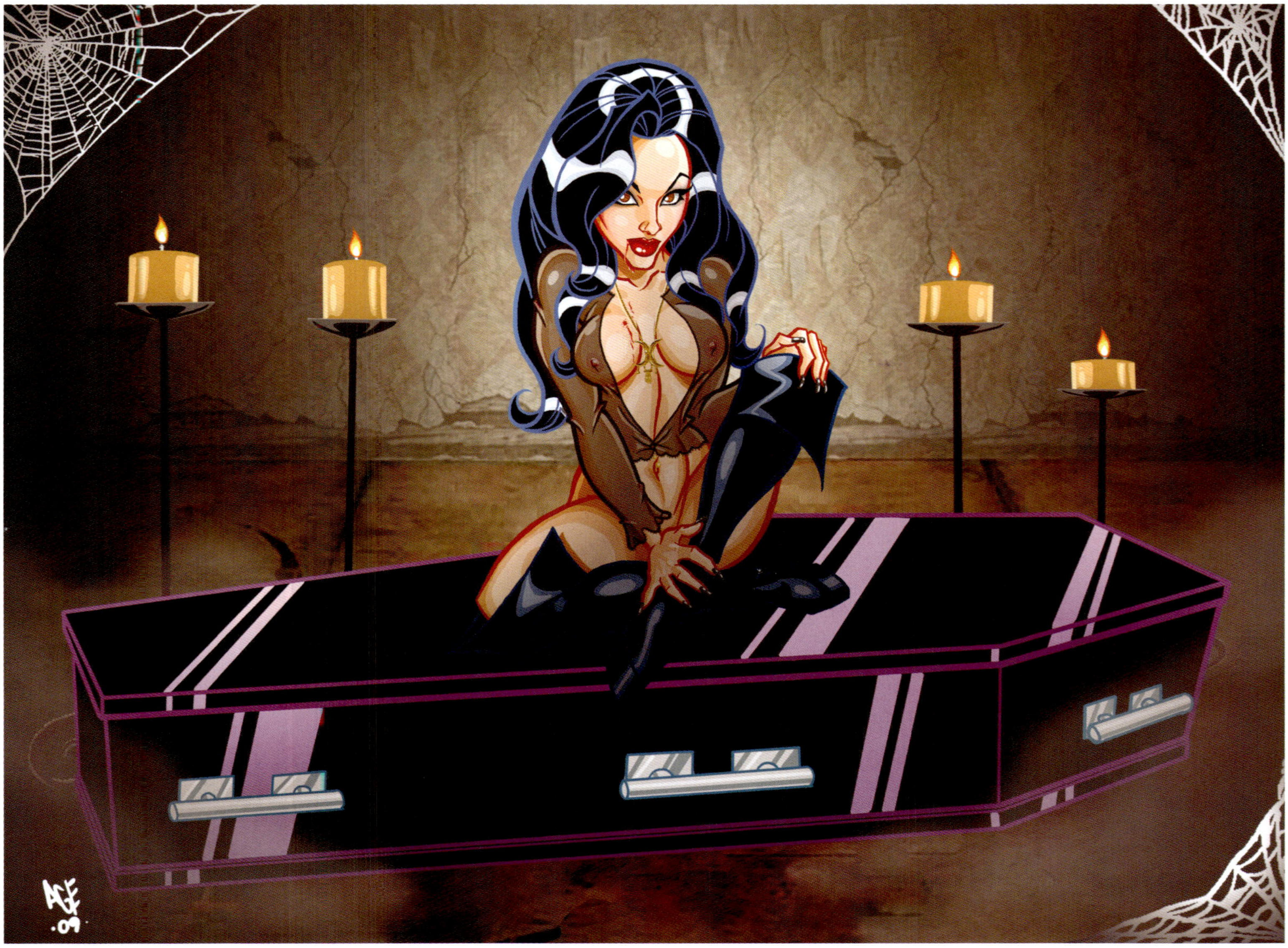

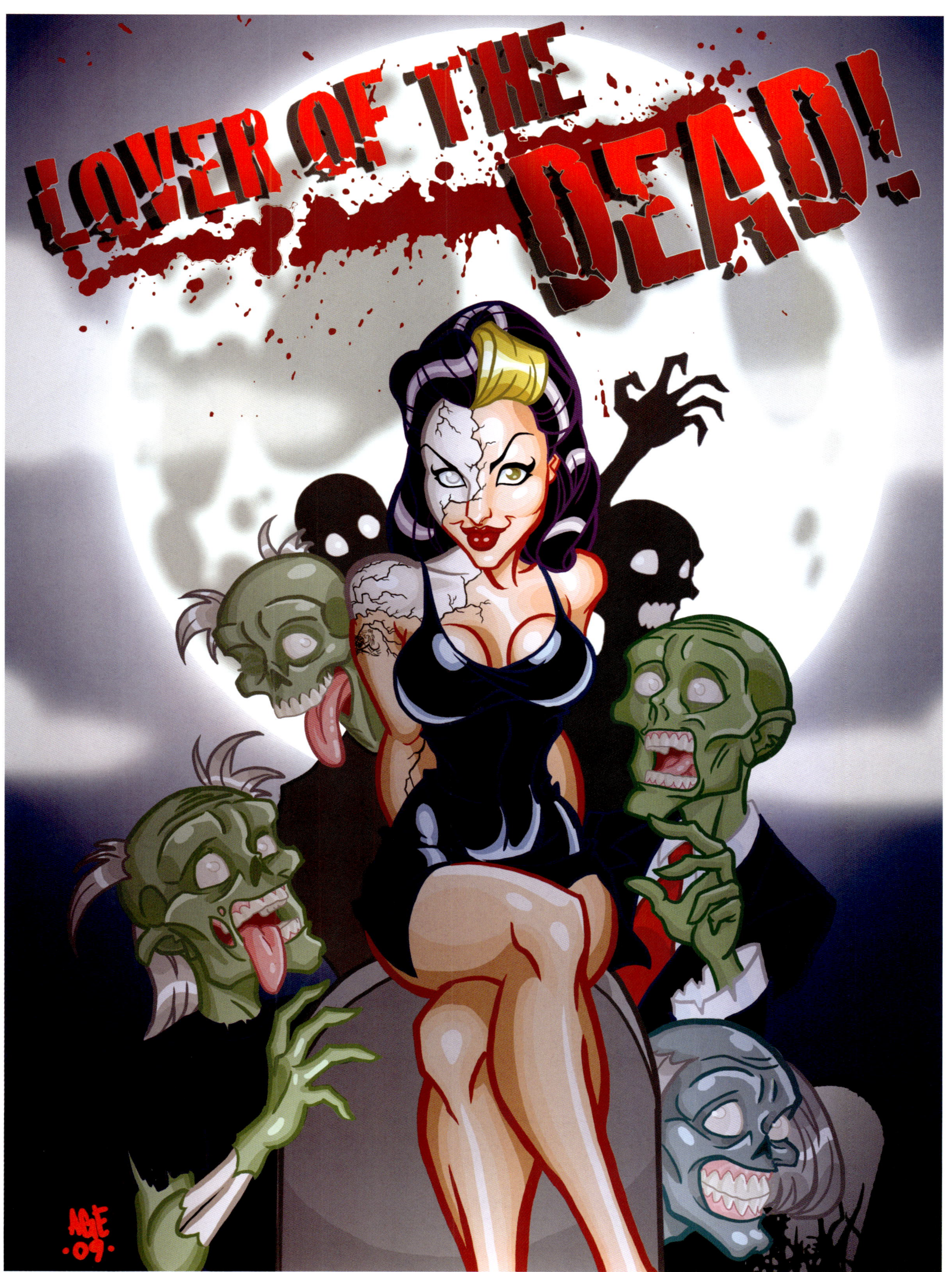
LOVER OF THE DEAD!
AGE
·09·

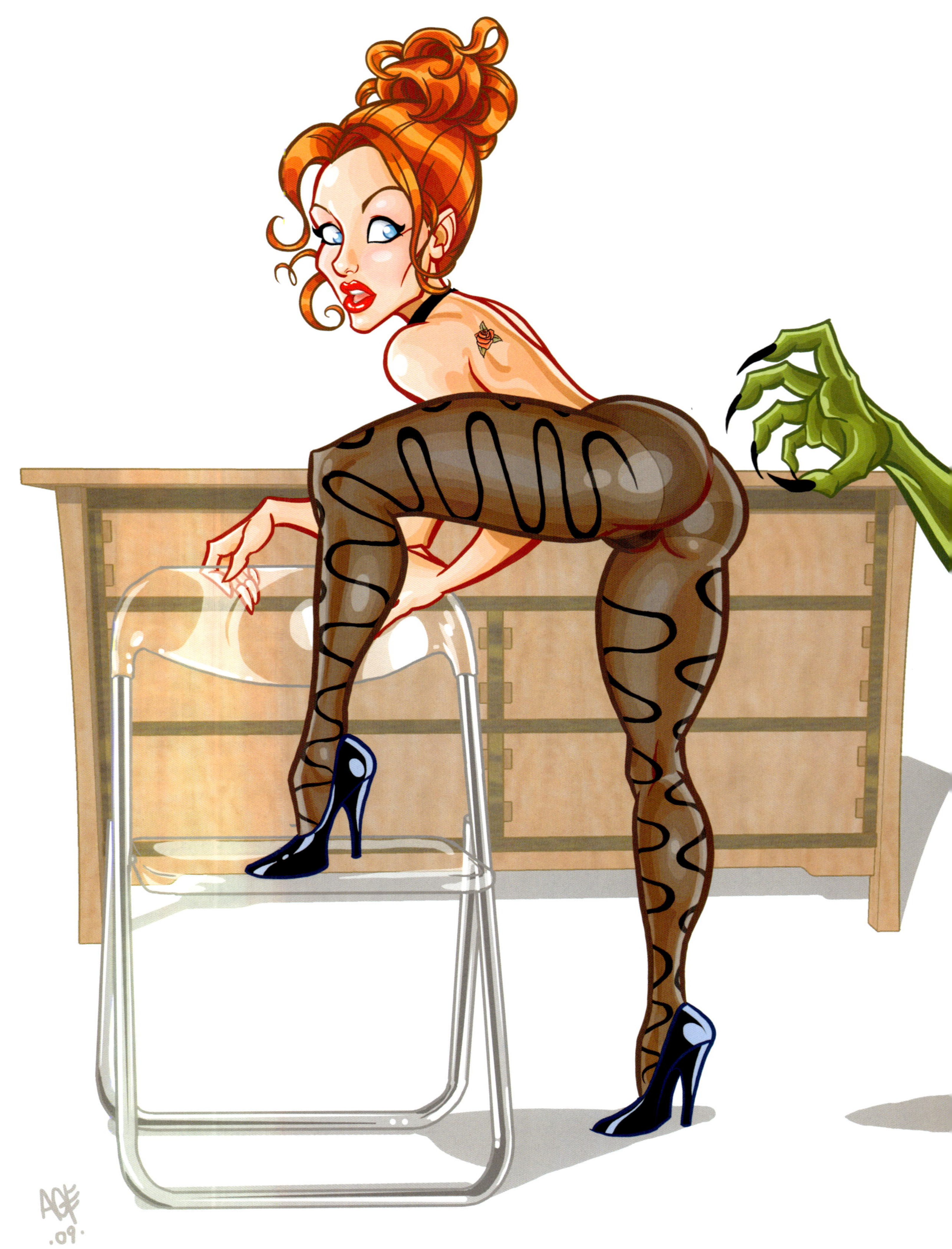
AGF
·09·

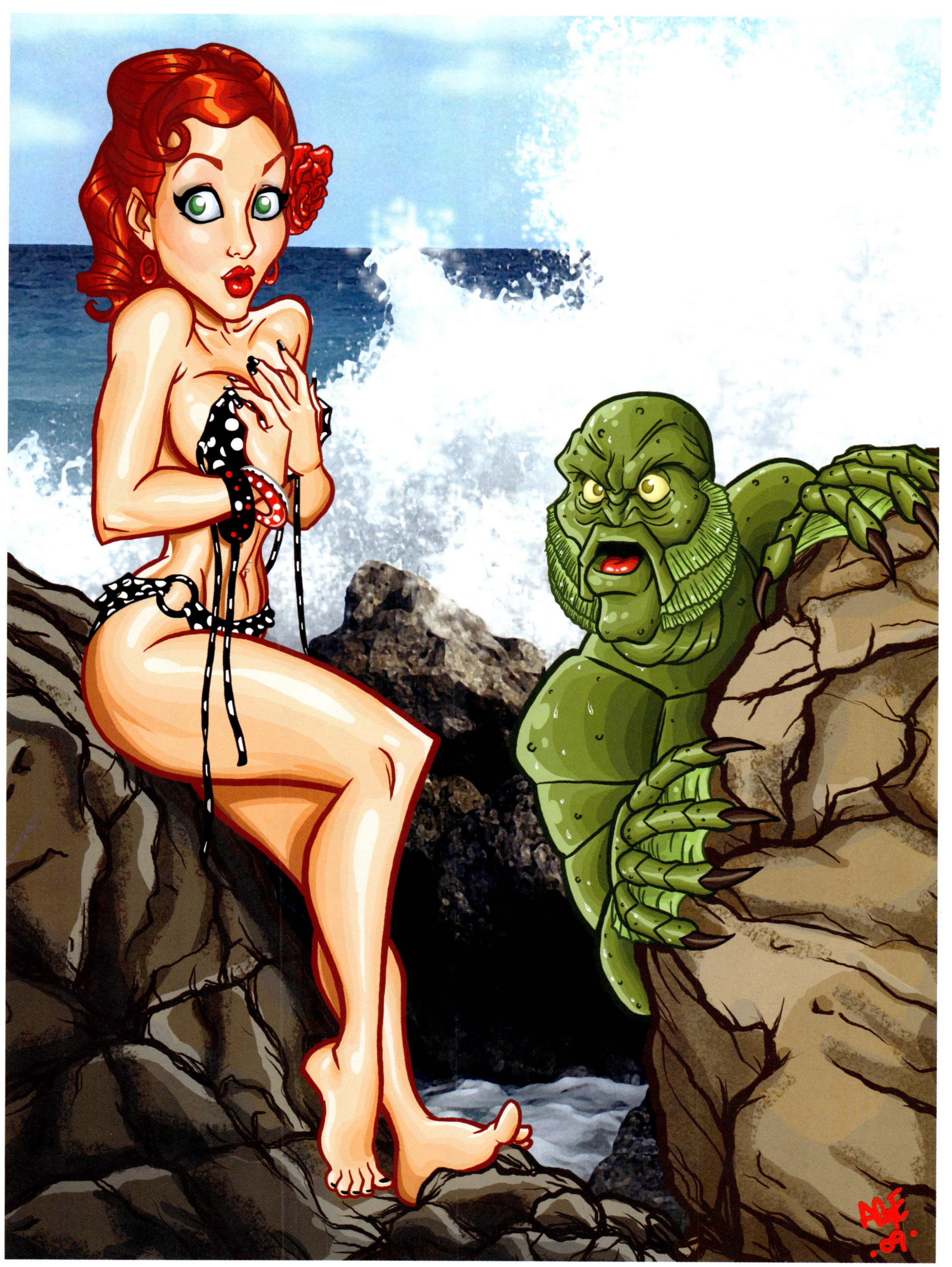
ADE
.09.

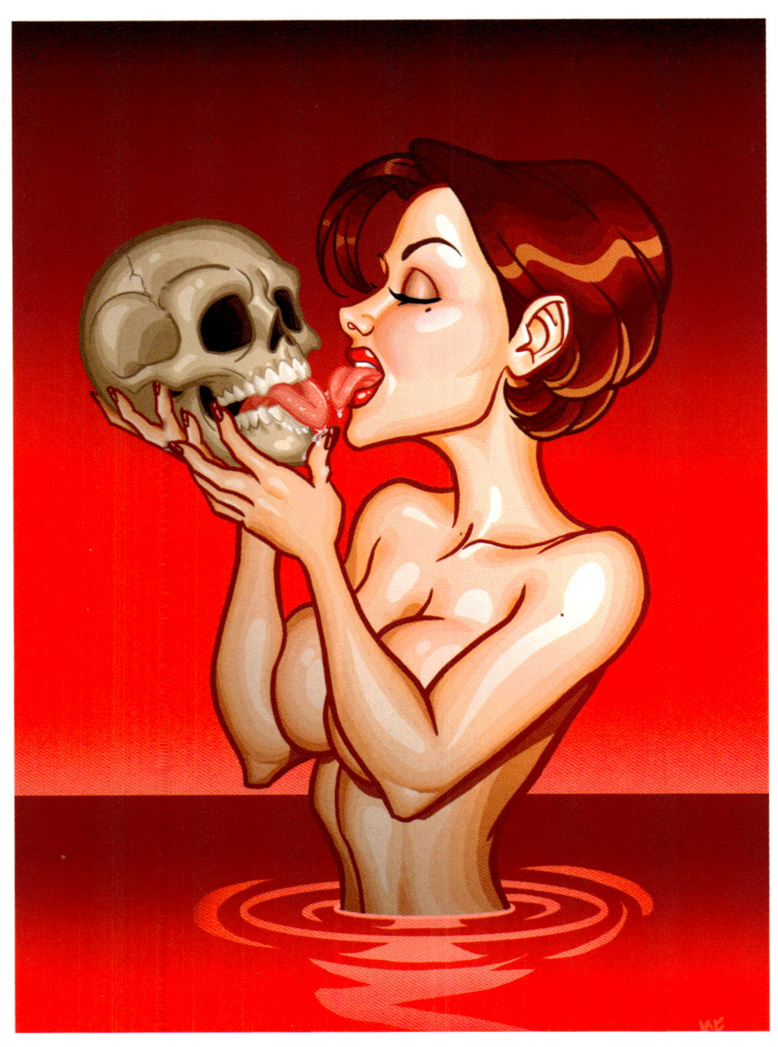

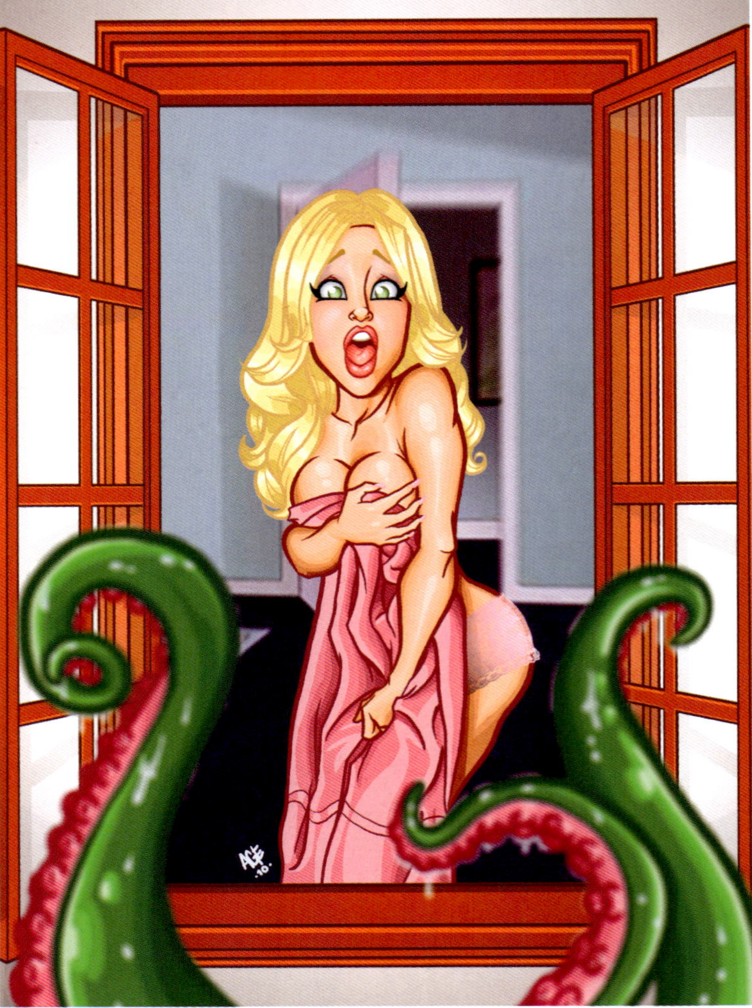

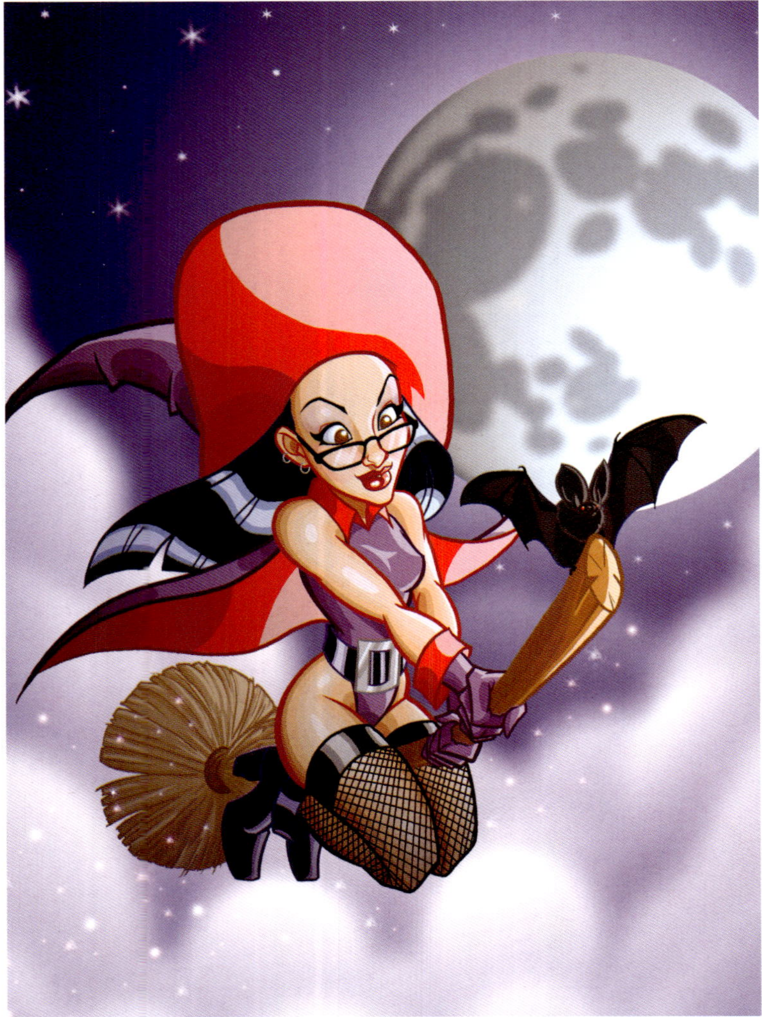

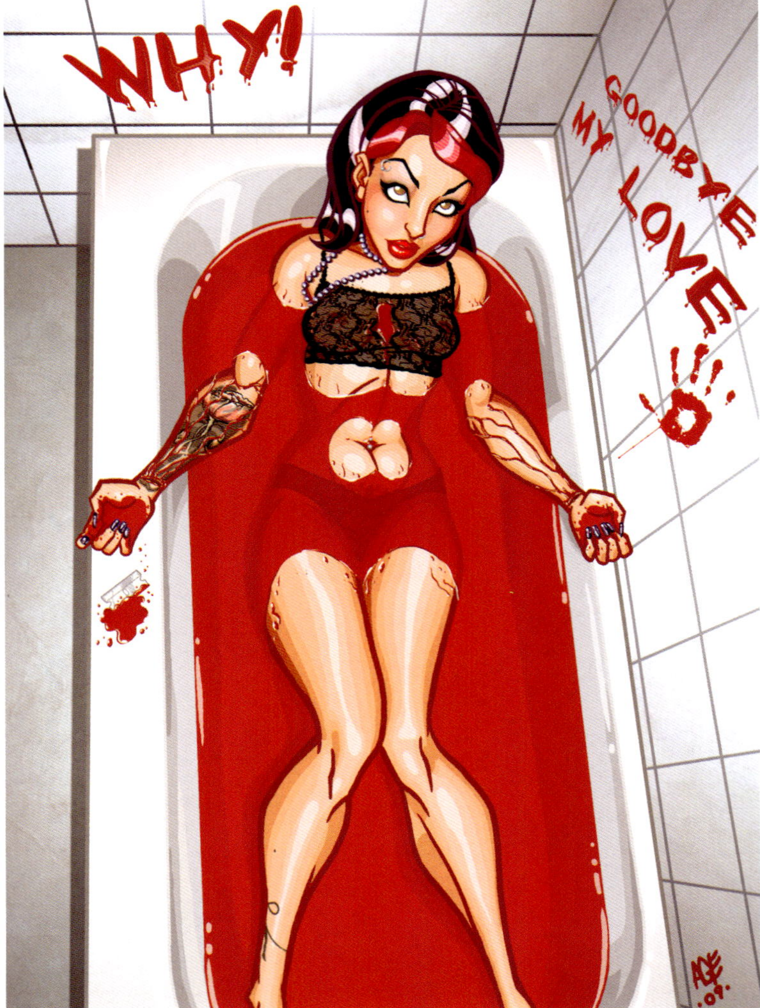

WHY!
GOODBYE
MY LOVE!!!

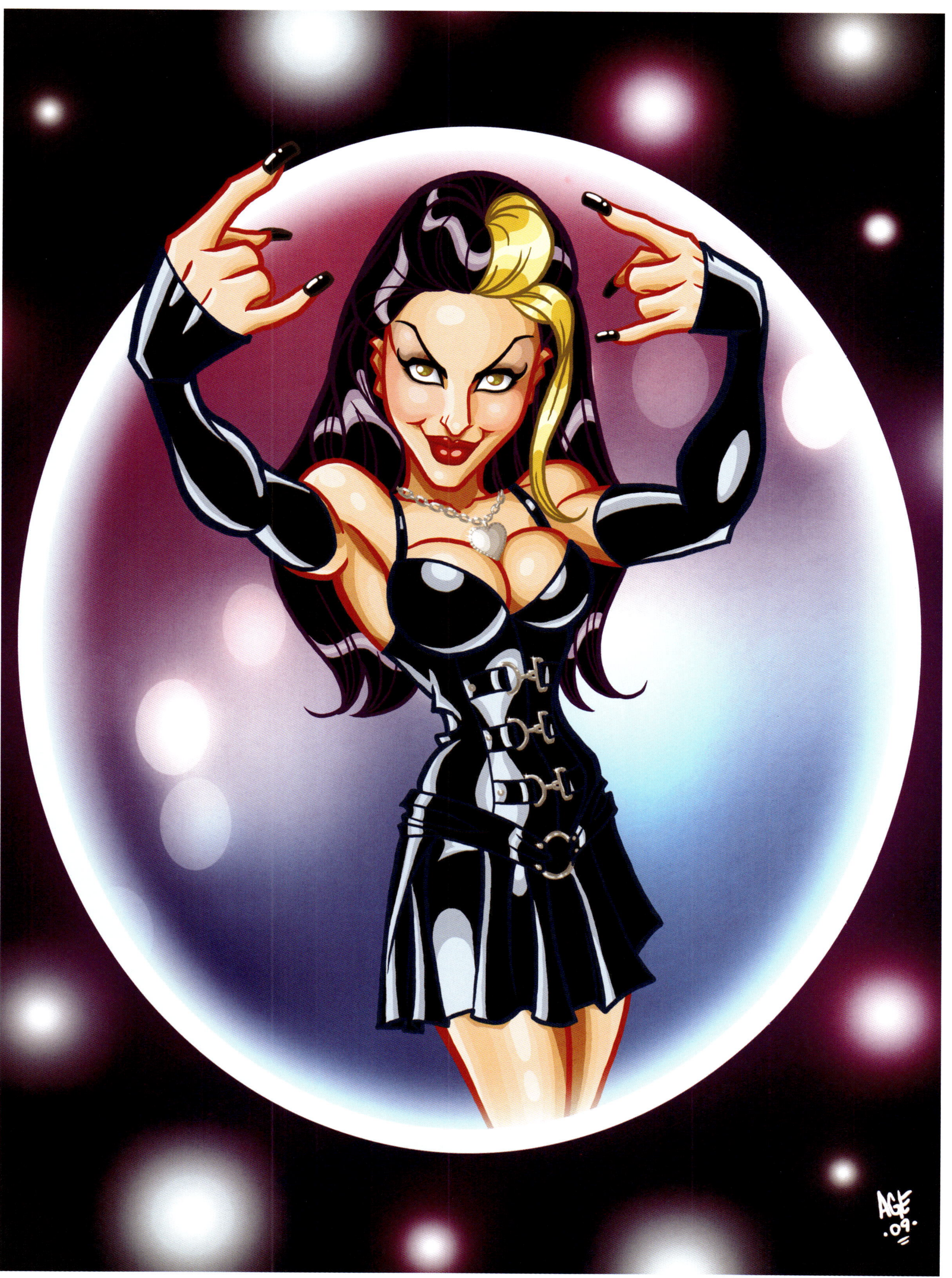
AGE
09

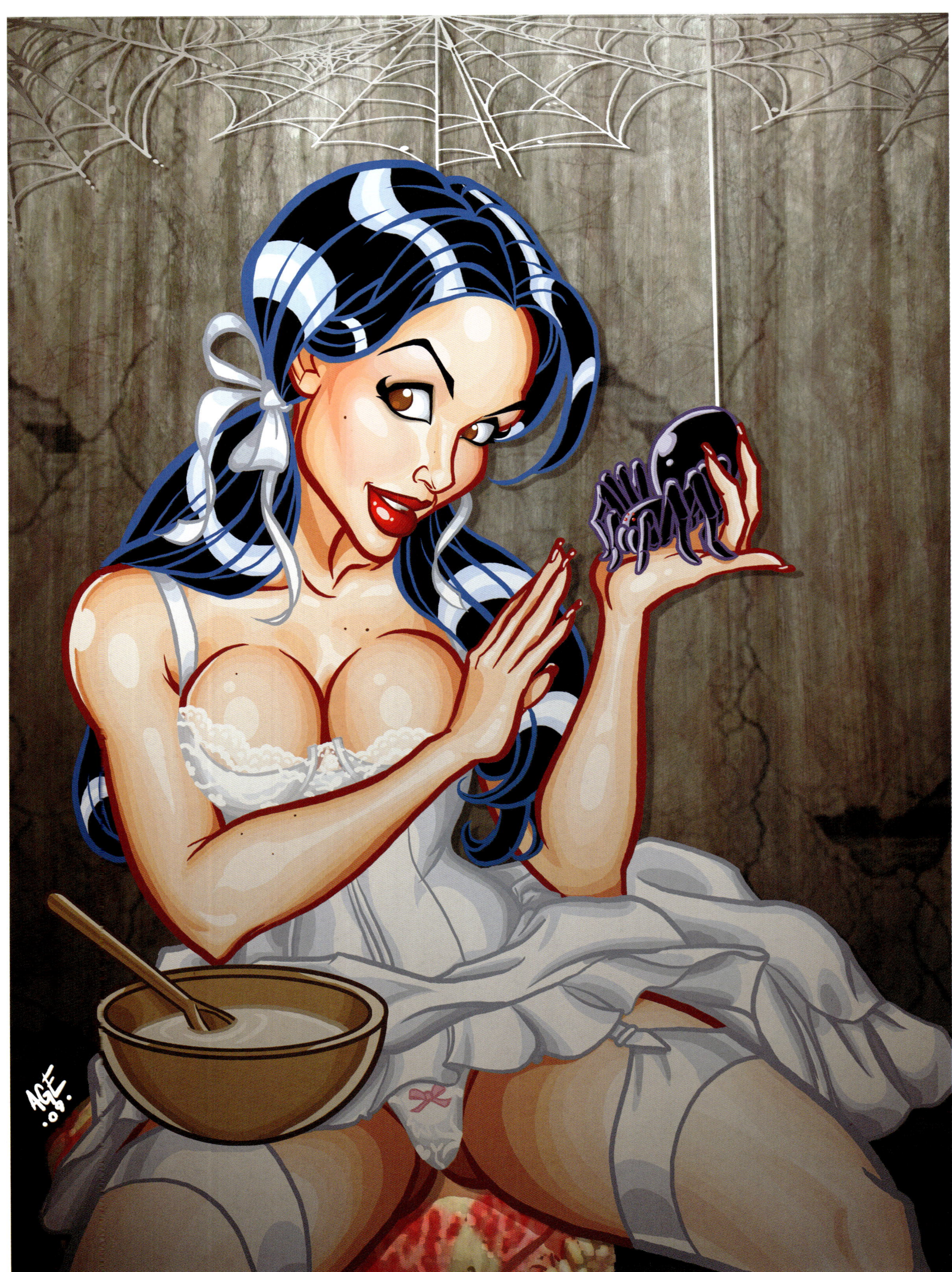

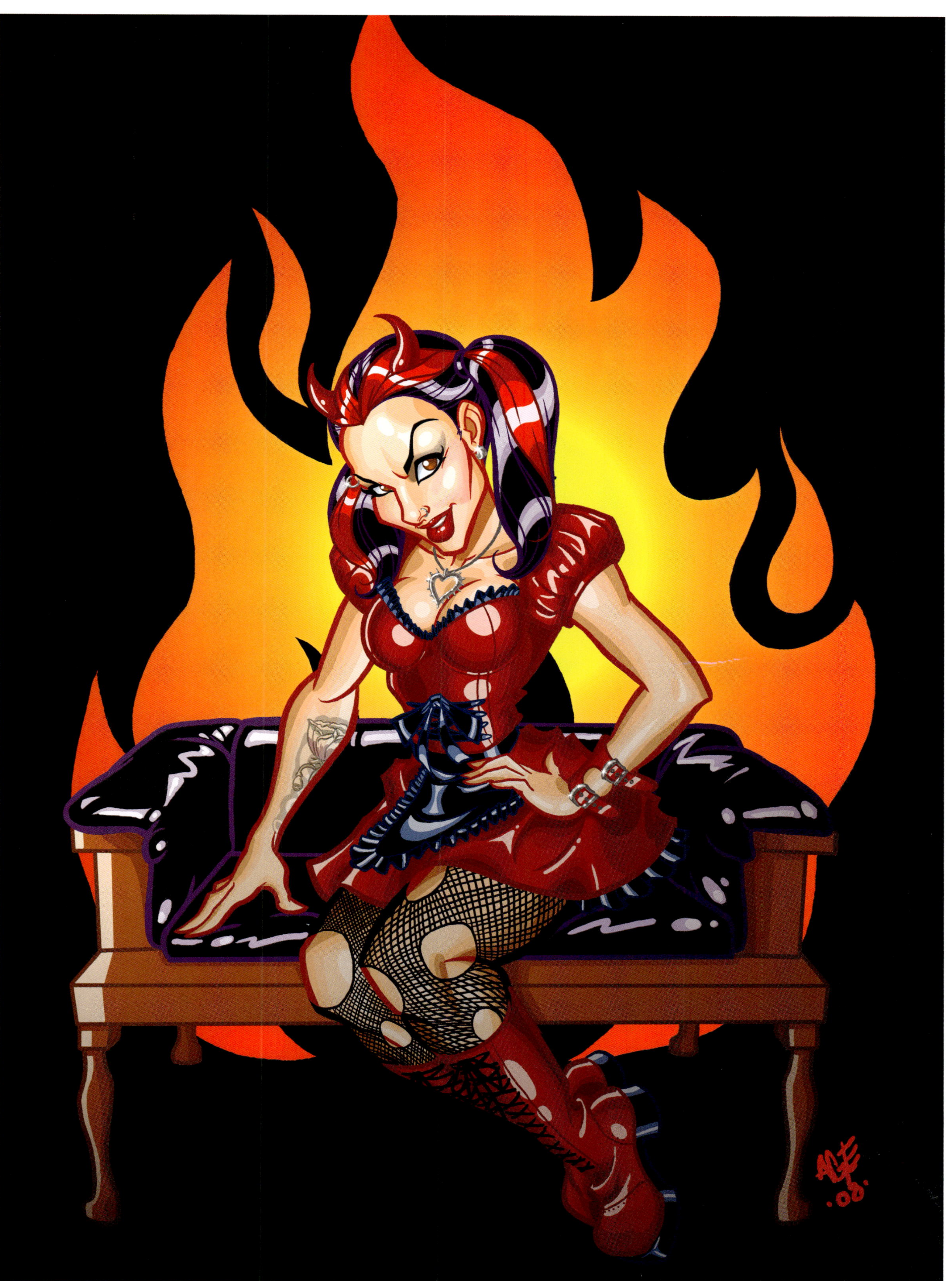

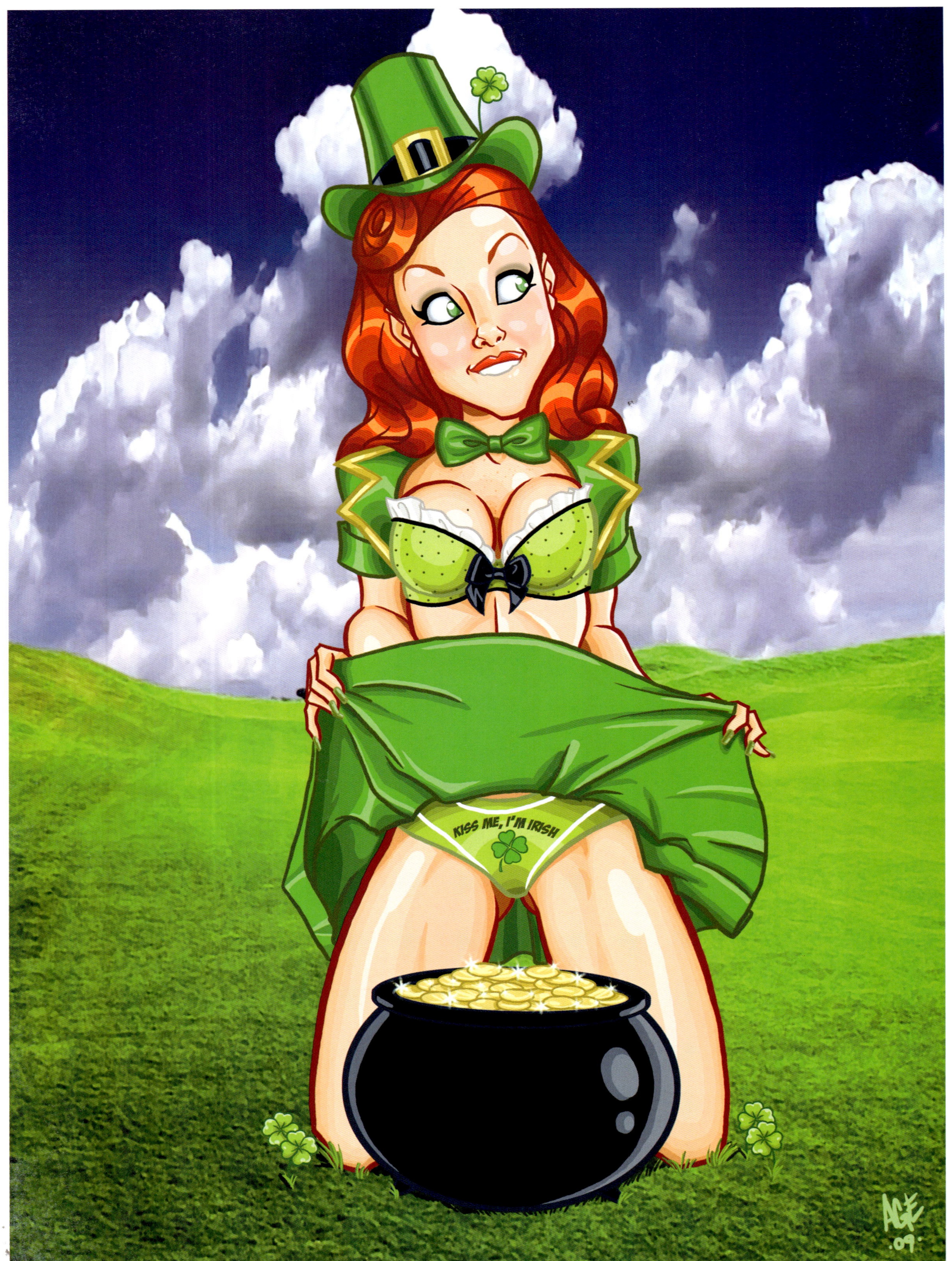
KISS ME, I'M IRISH
ACE
.09.

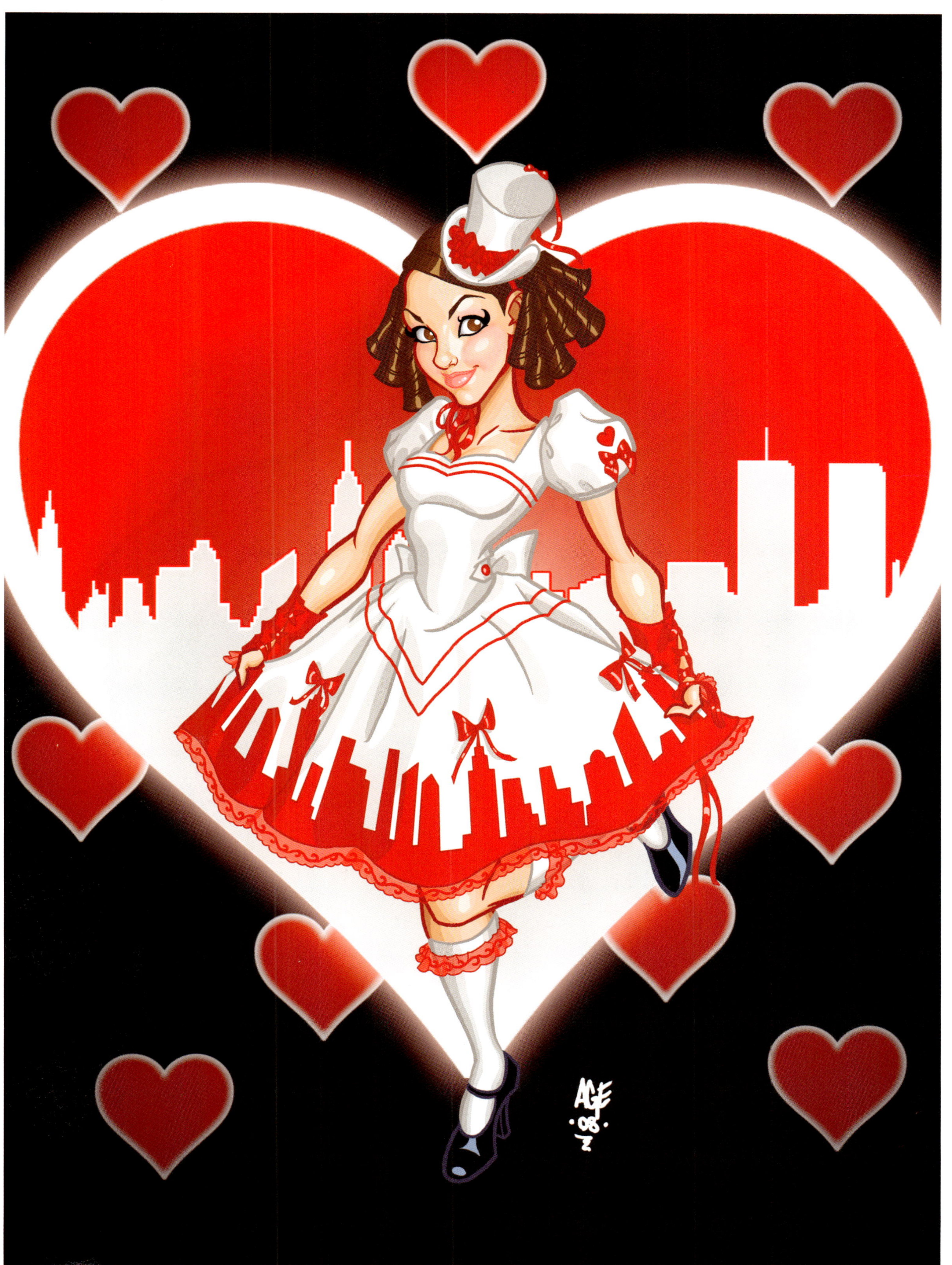
AGE
08

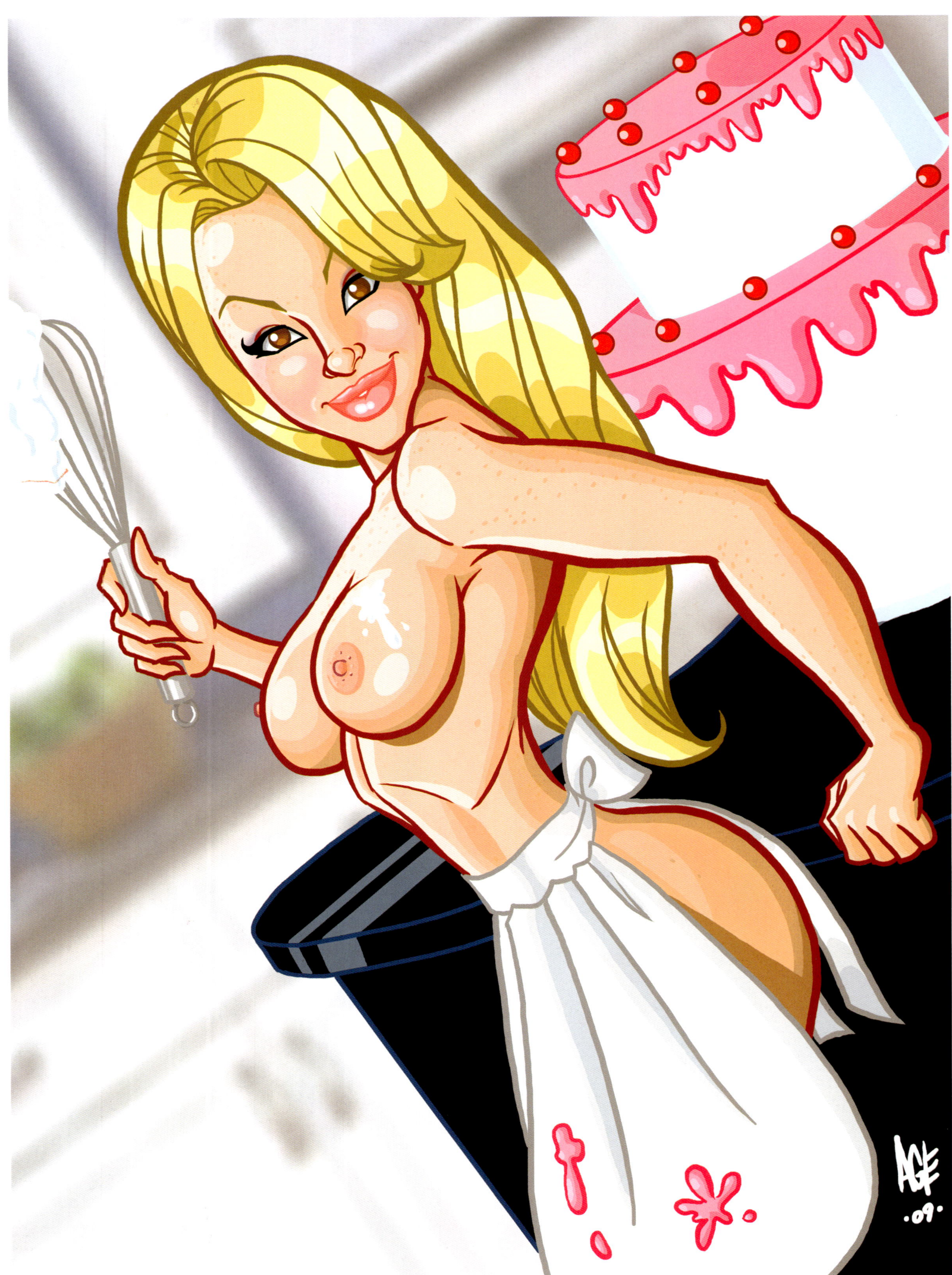

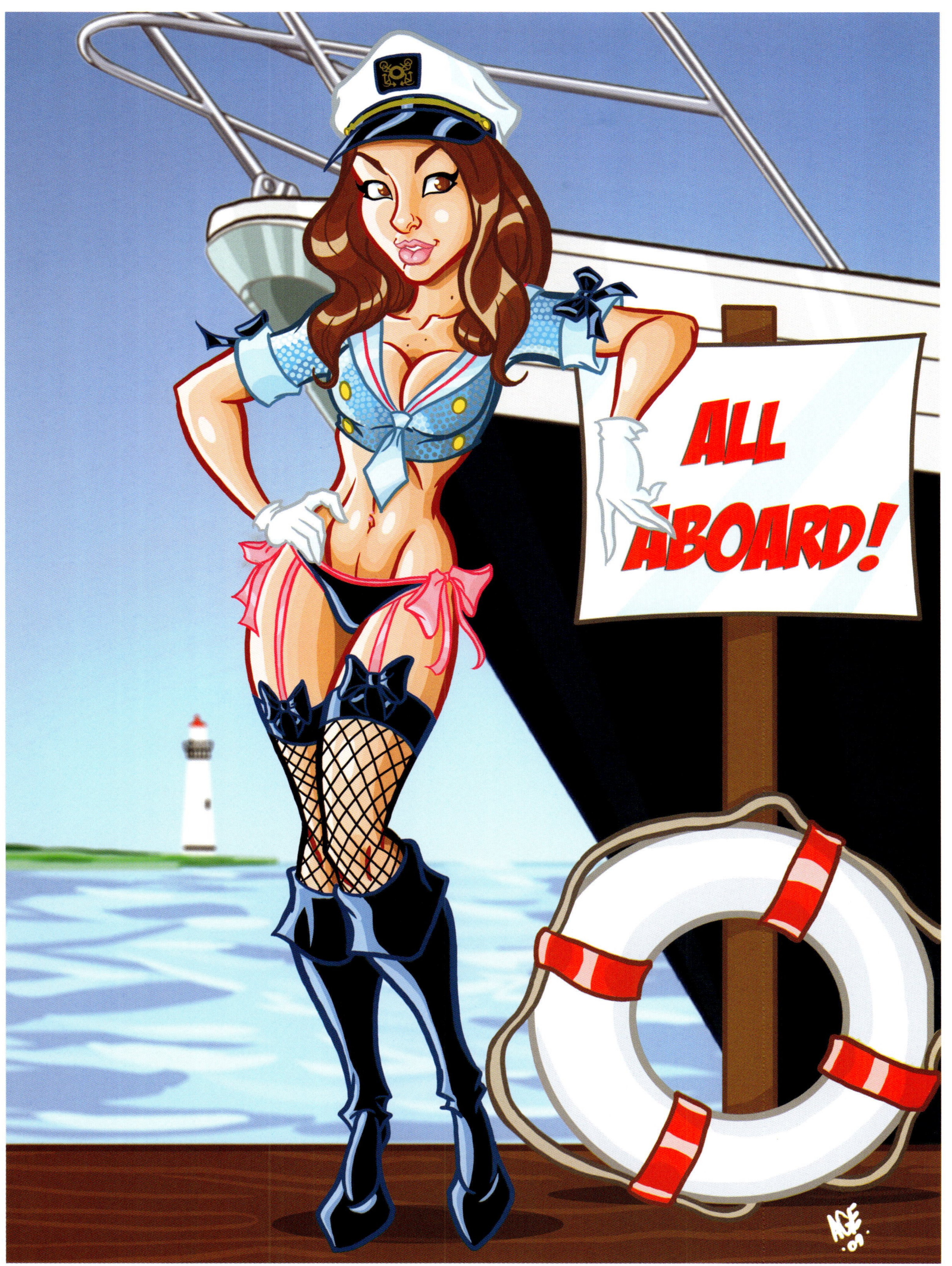
ALL ABOARD!

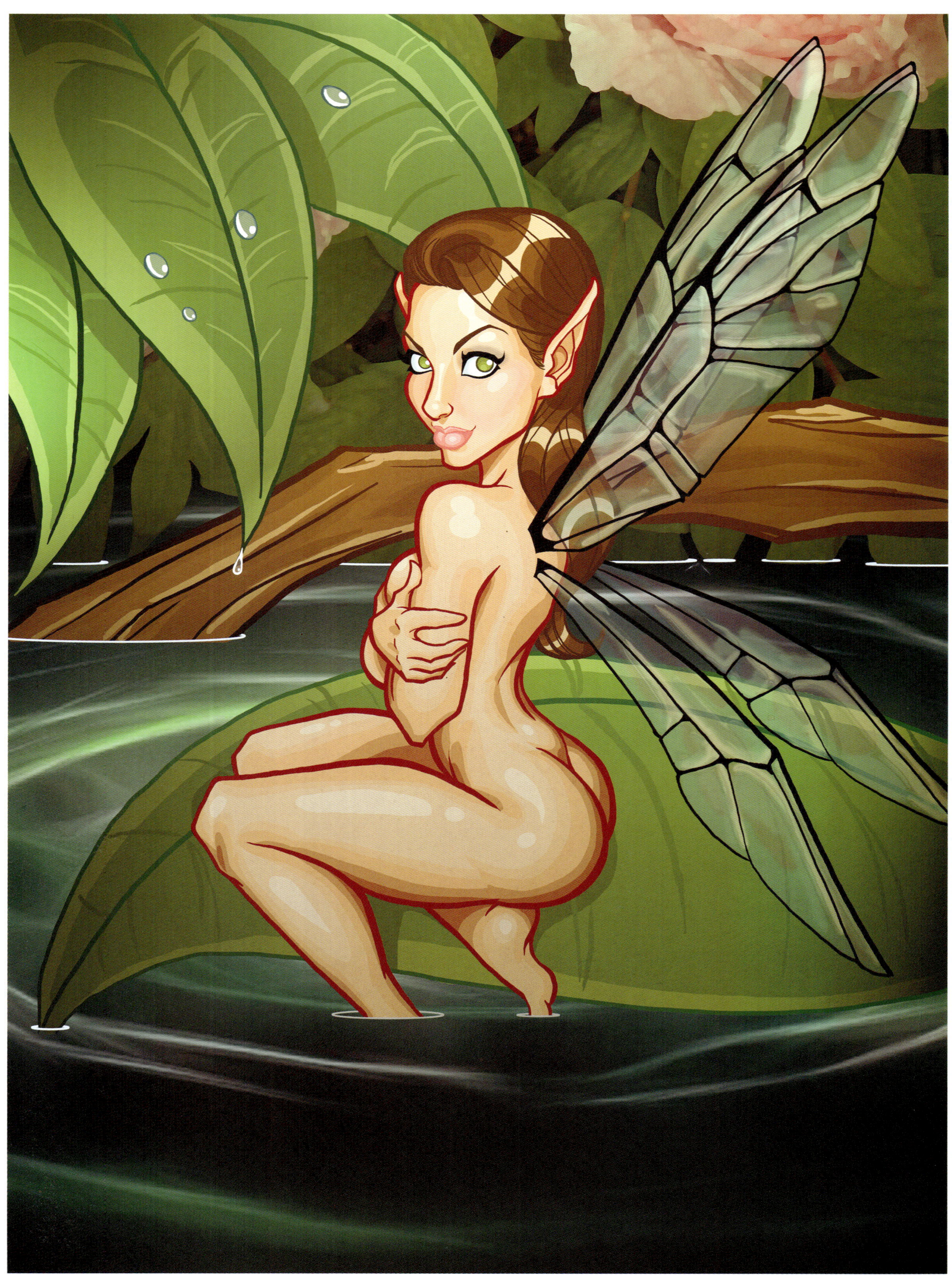

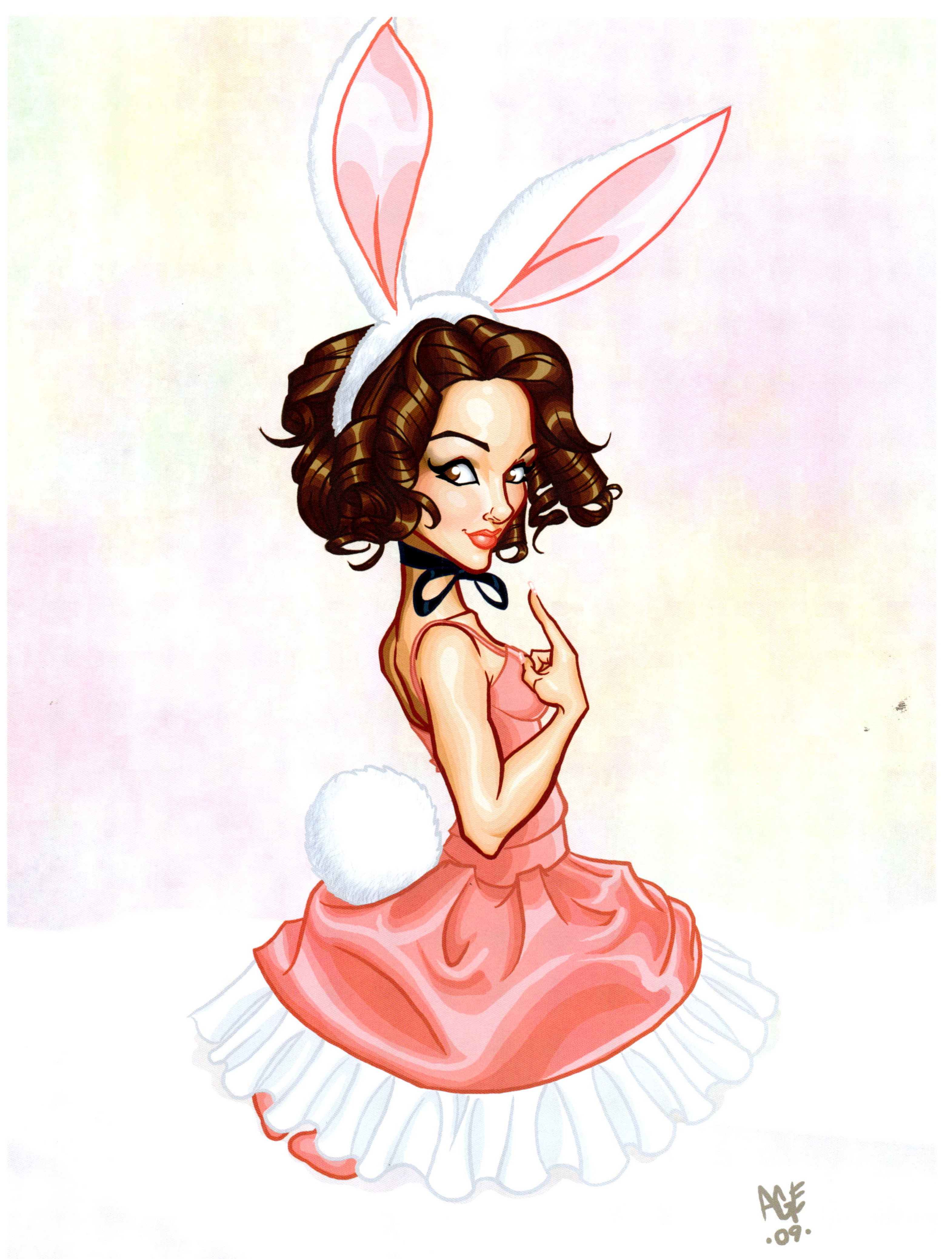
AGE
·09·

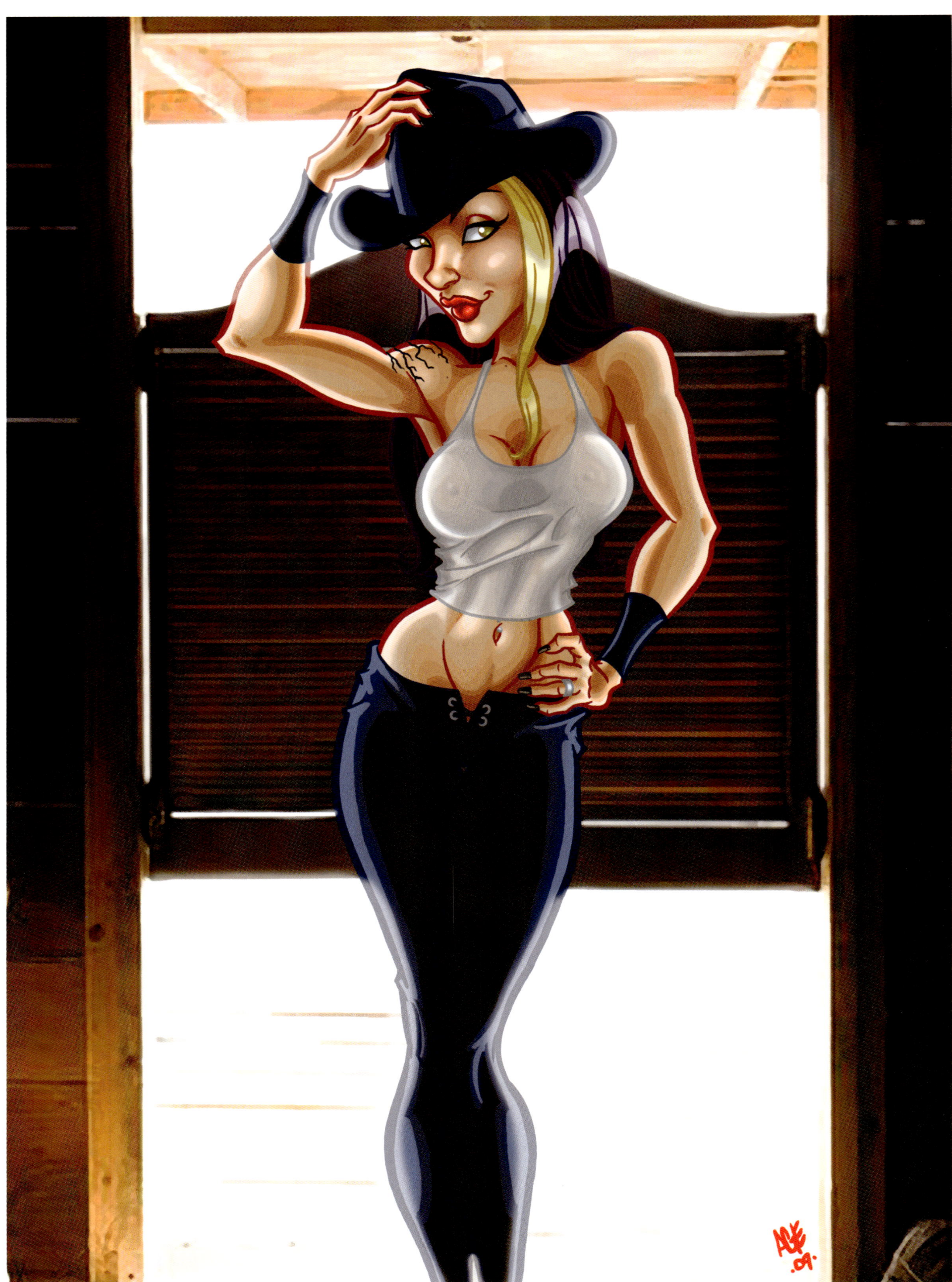

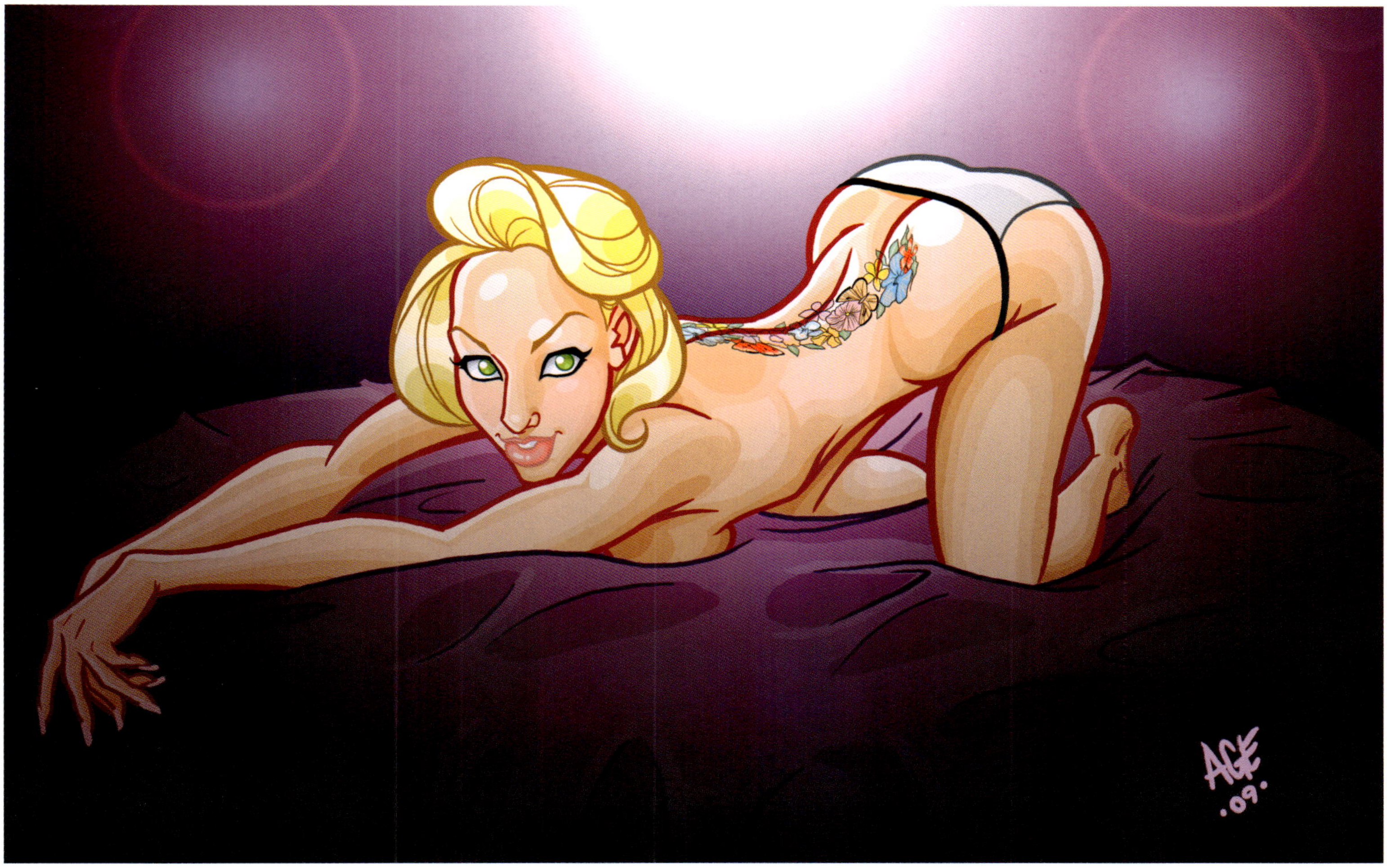

AGE '09

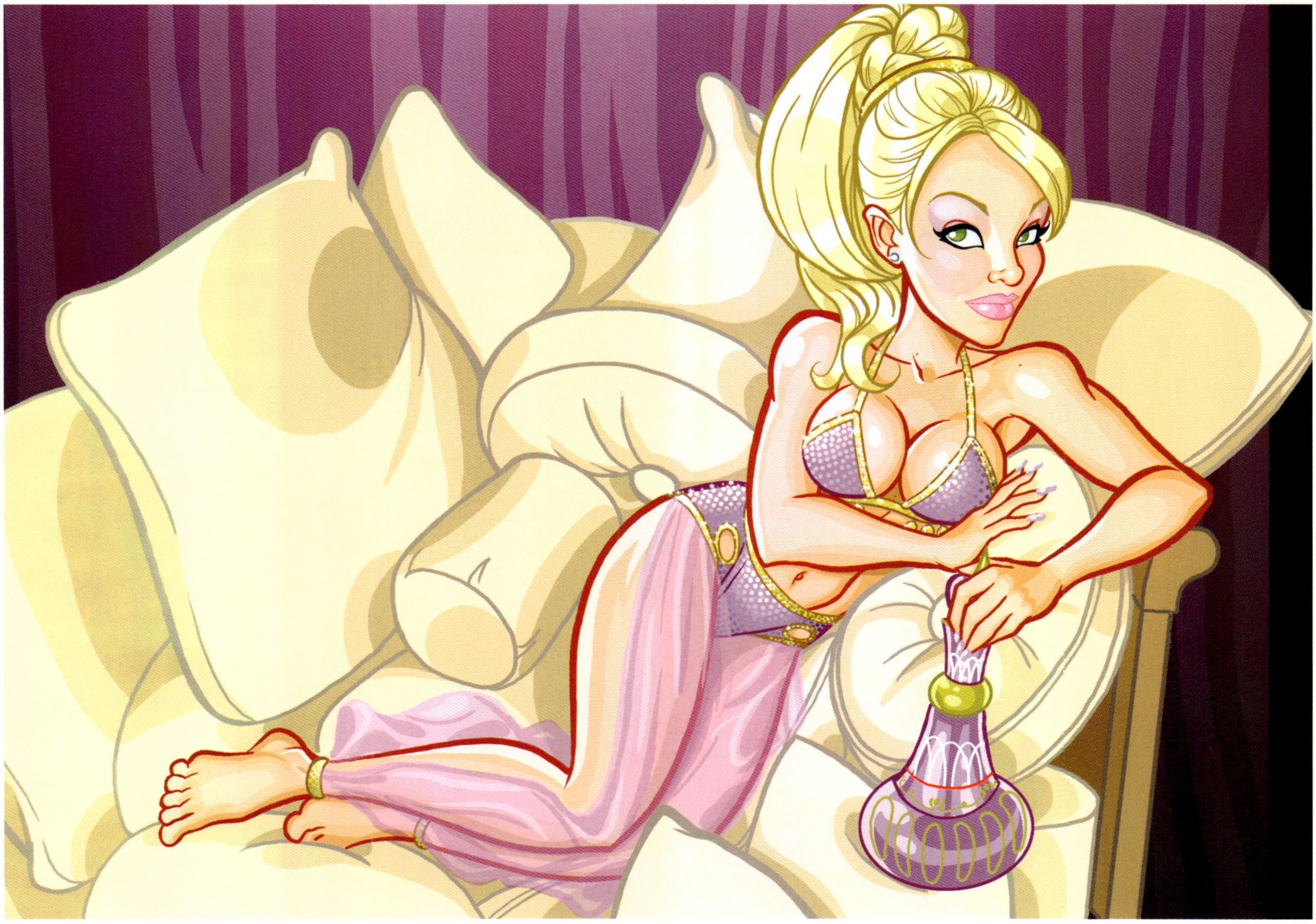

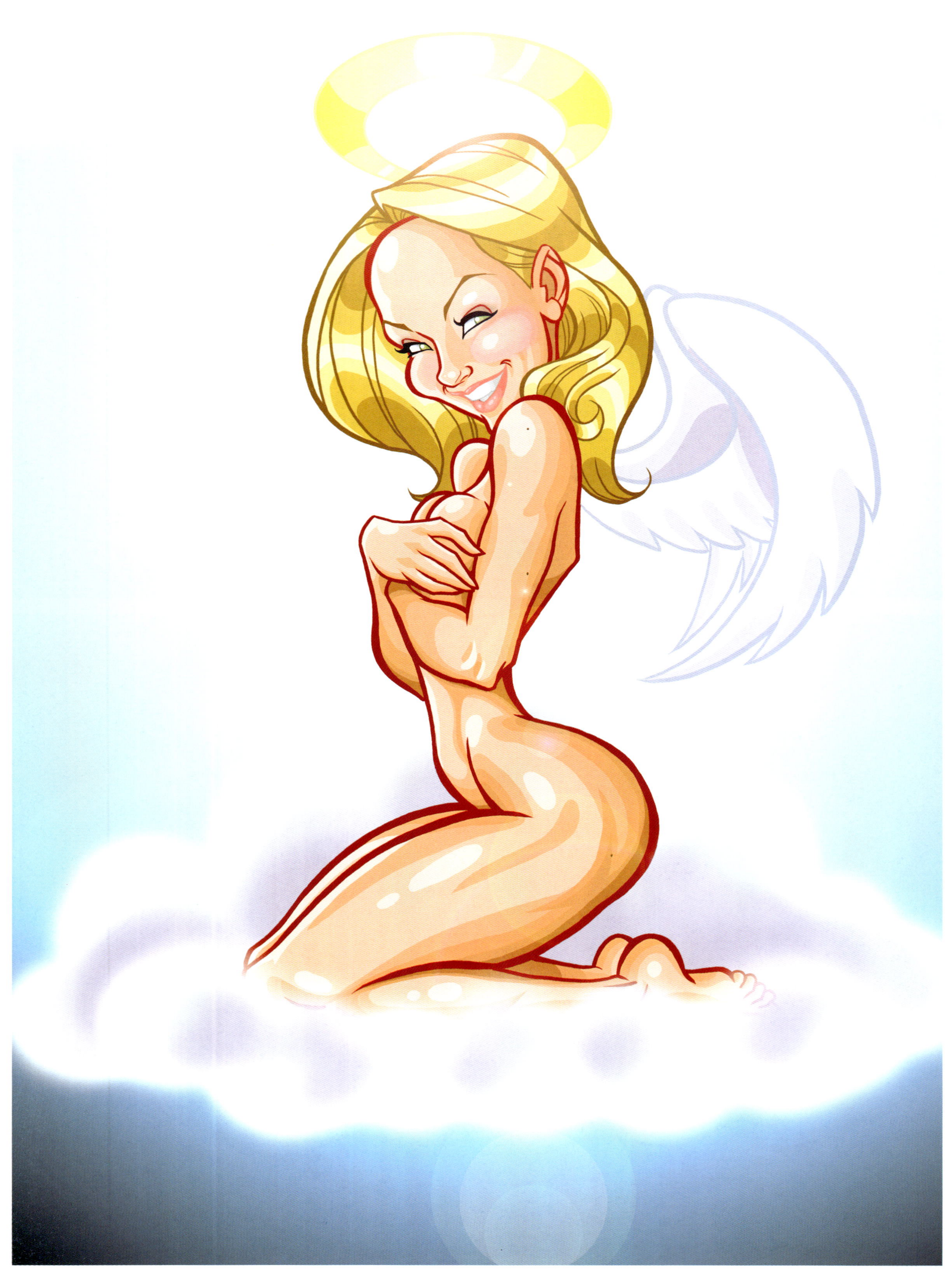

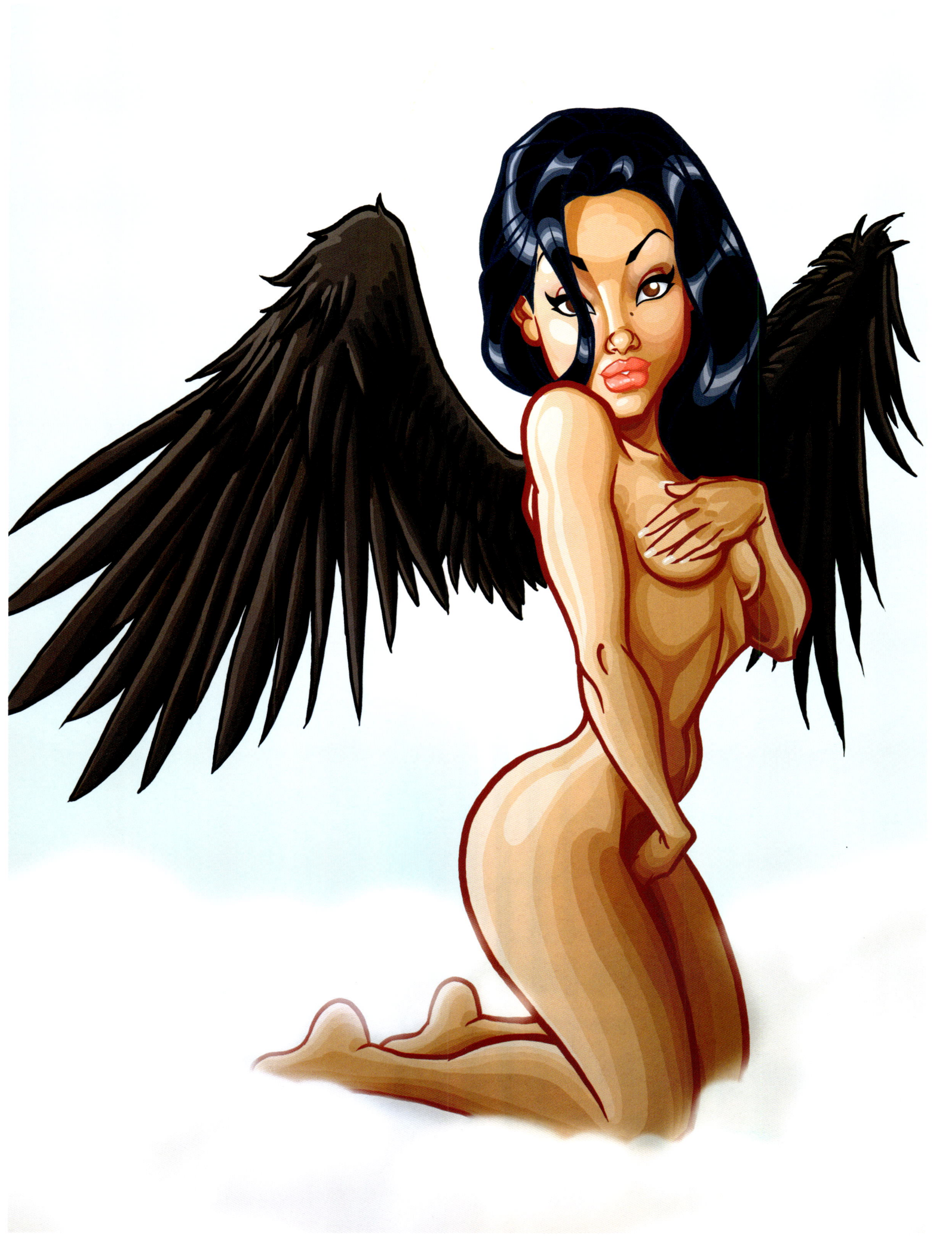

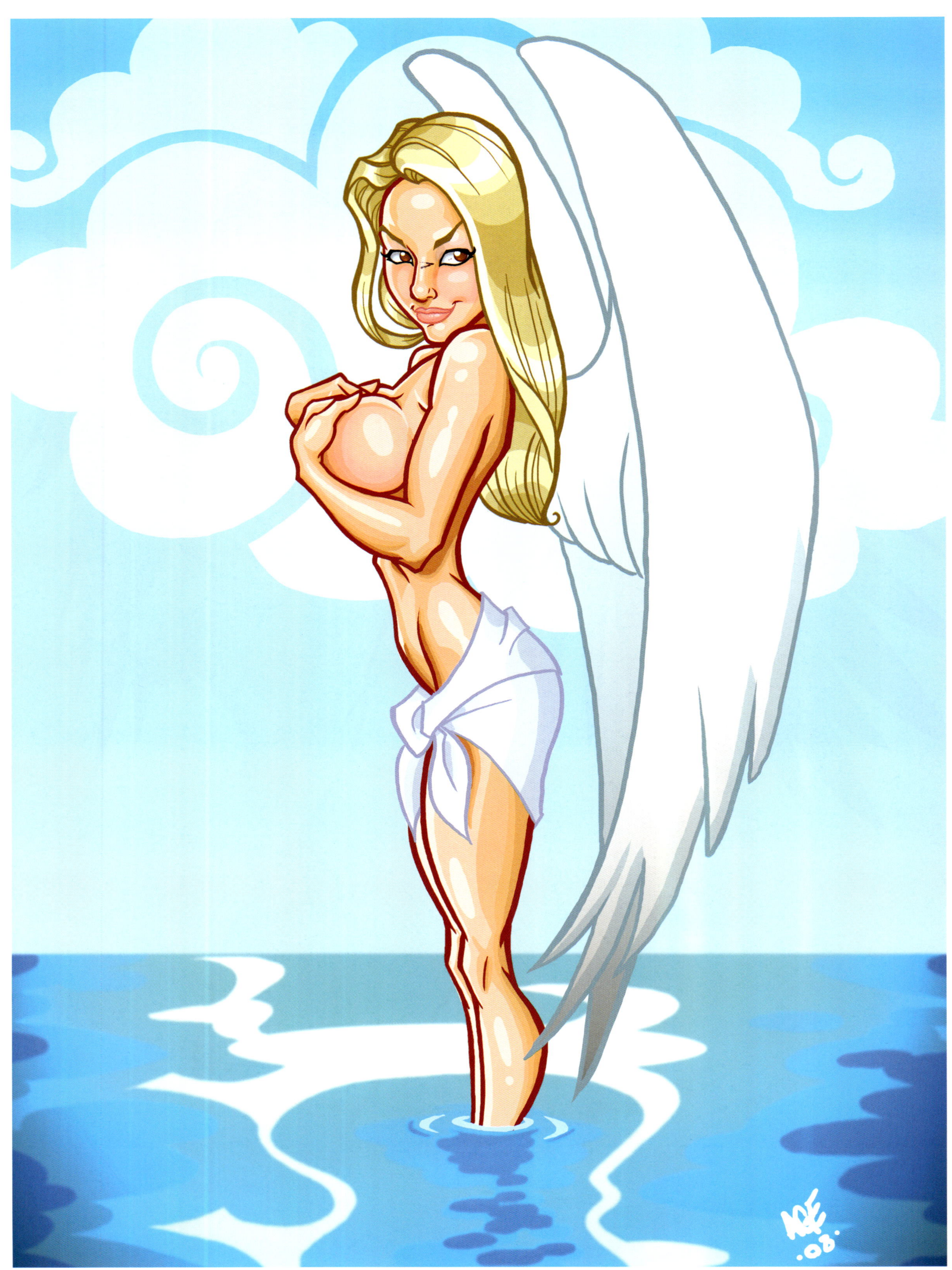
ACE
.08.

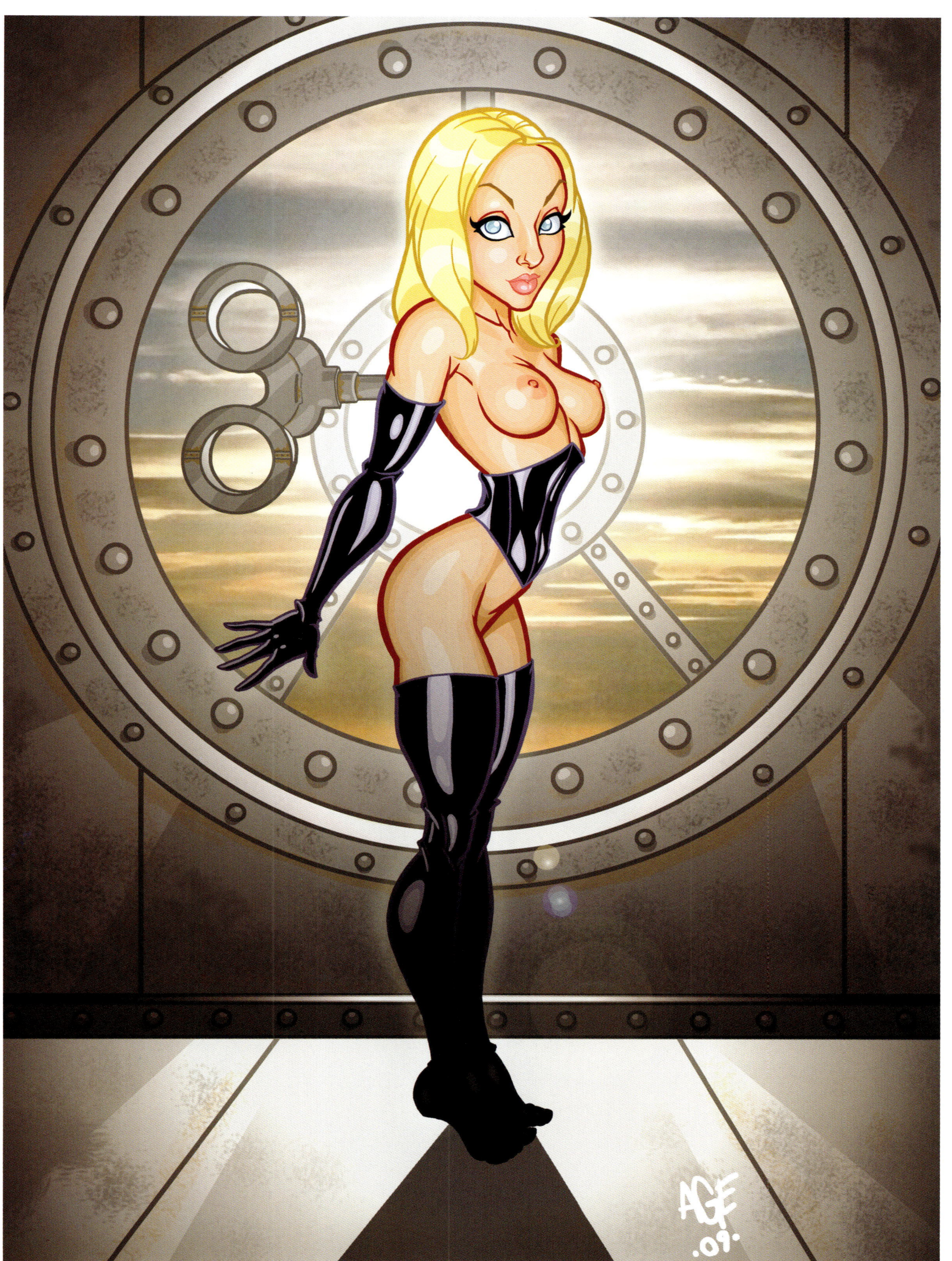
AGE
.09.

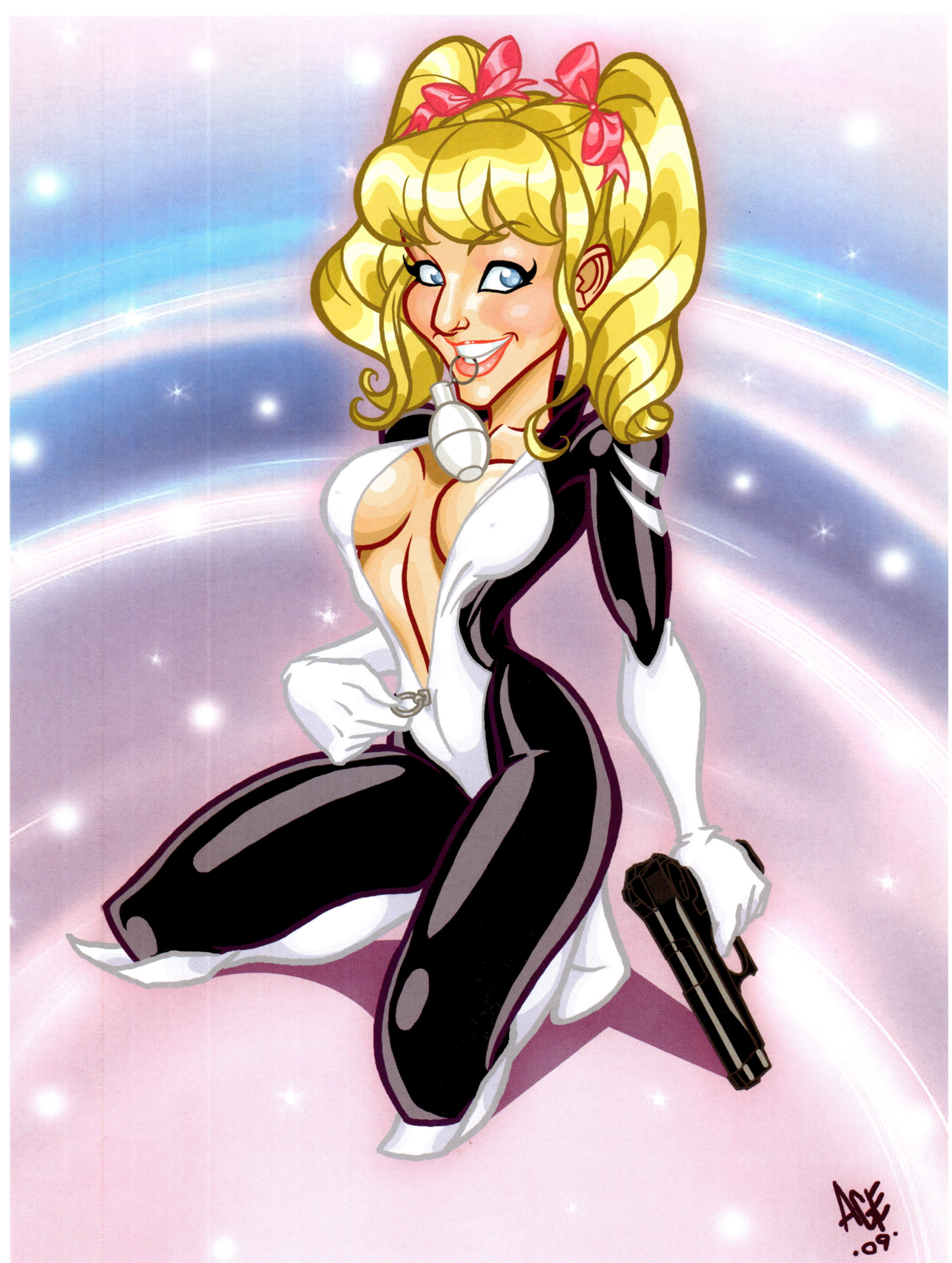
AGE
.09.

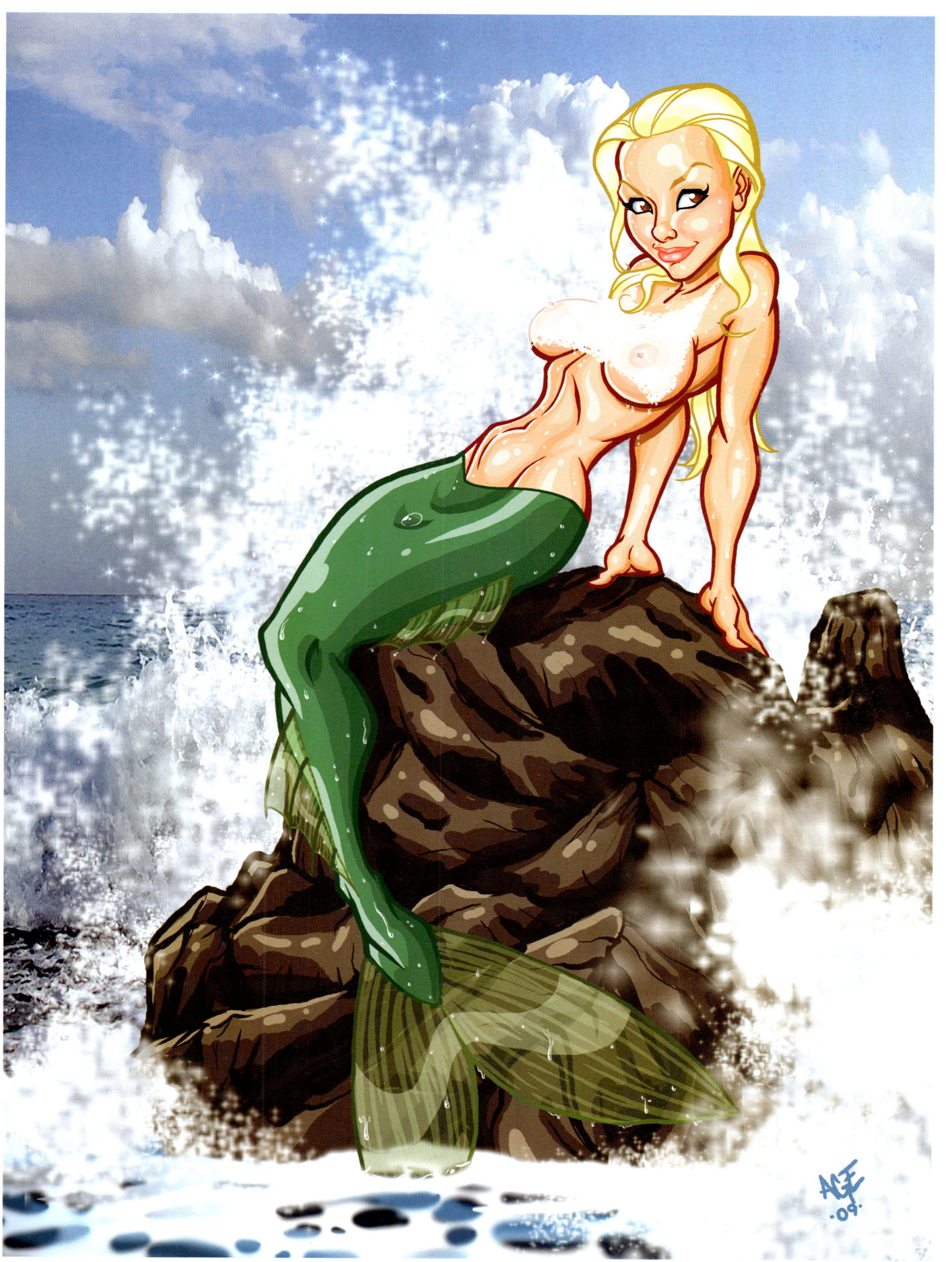
ACE
'09

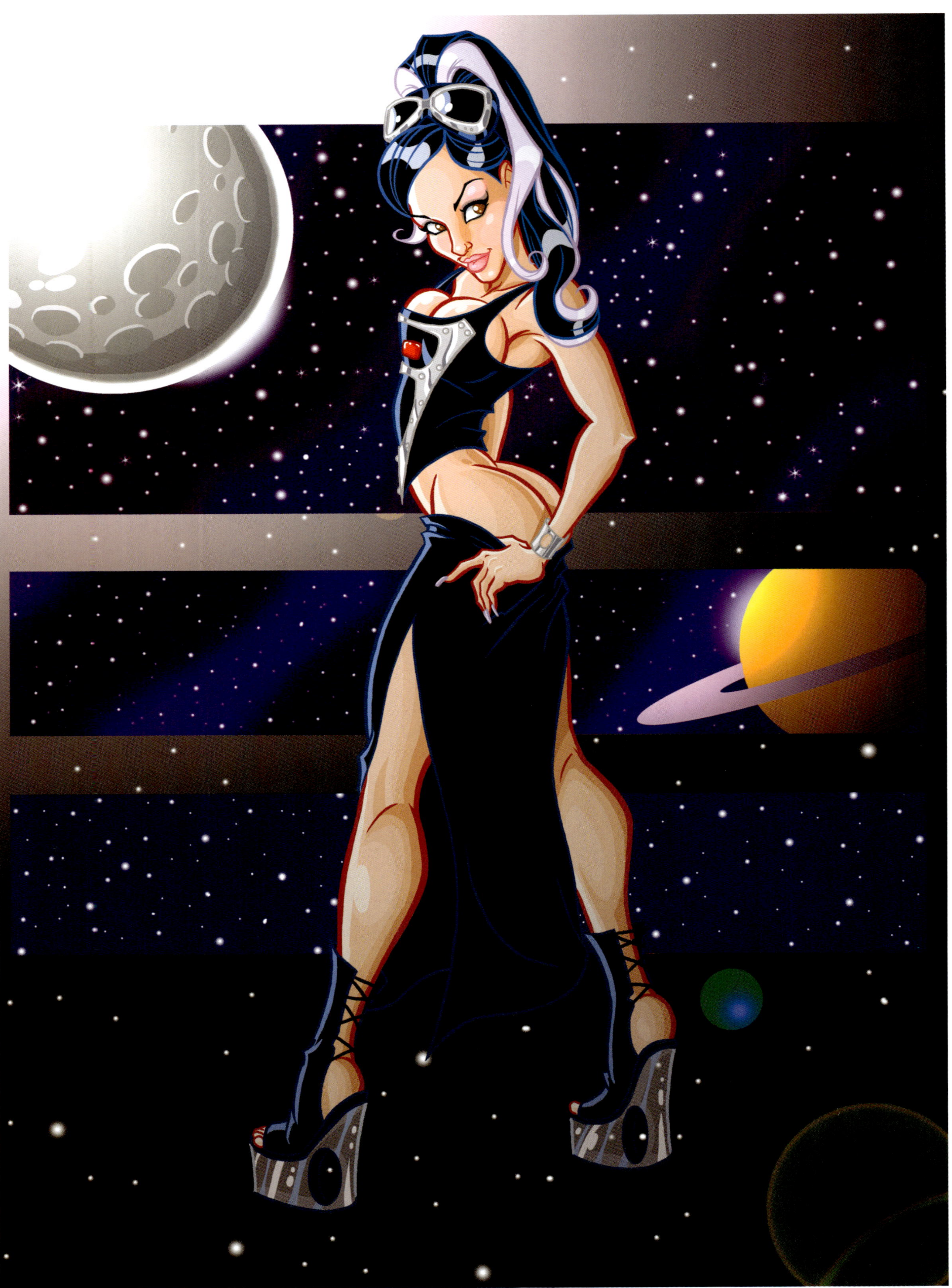

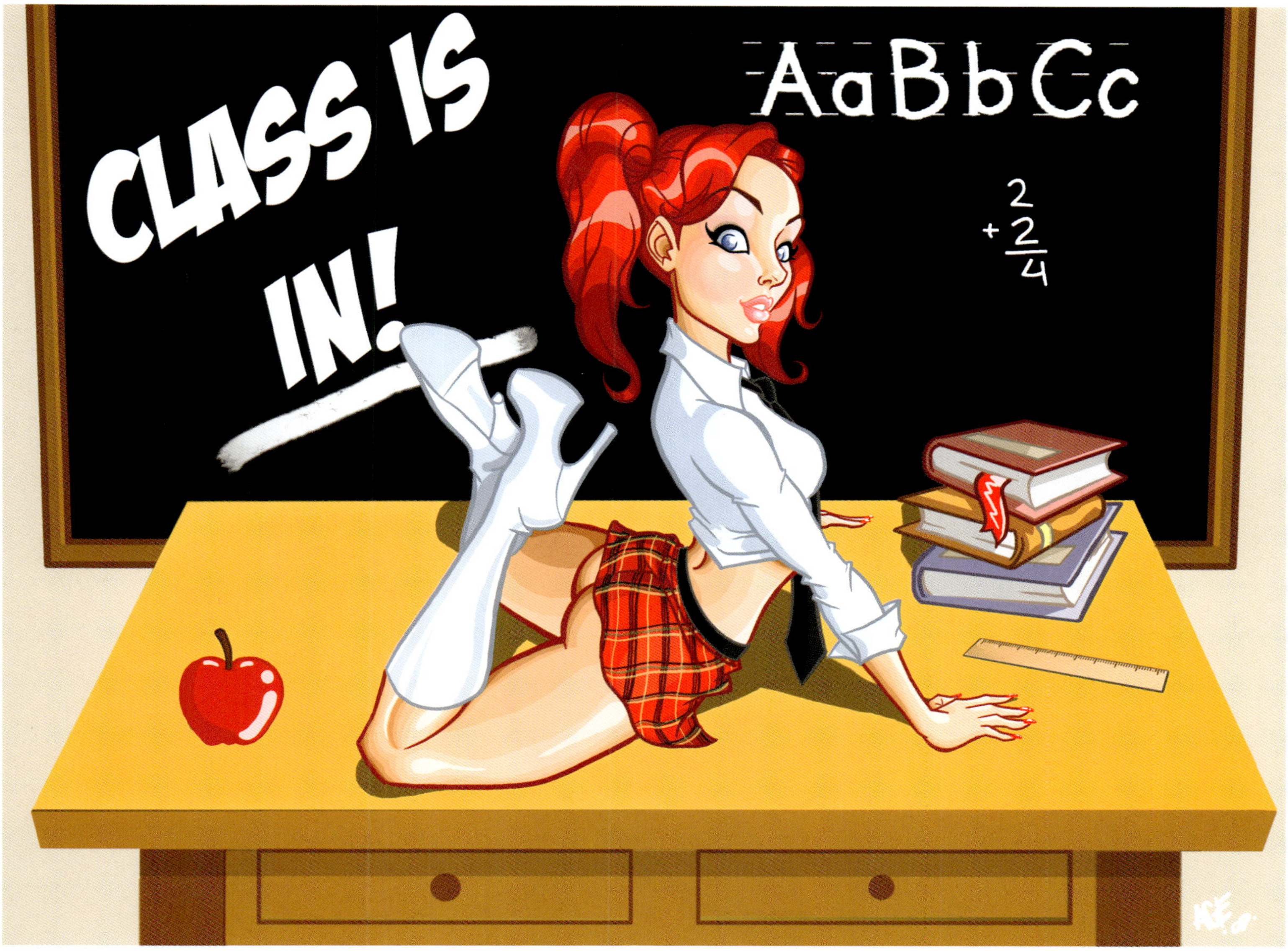

CLASS IS IN!
AaBbCc
2
+2
4

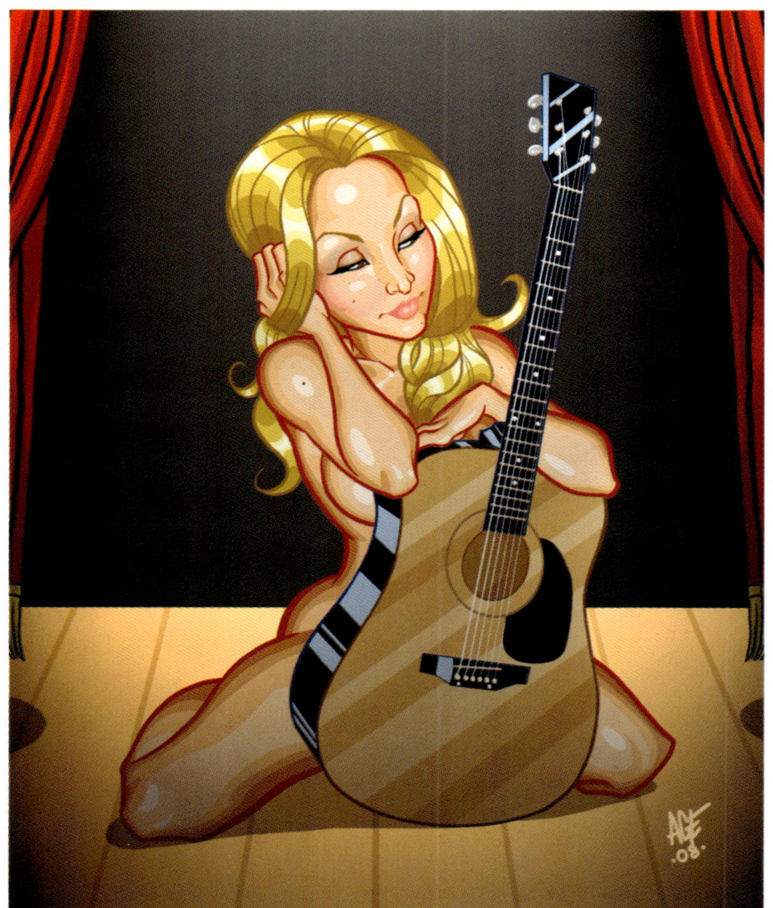

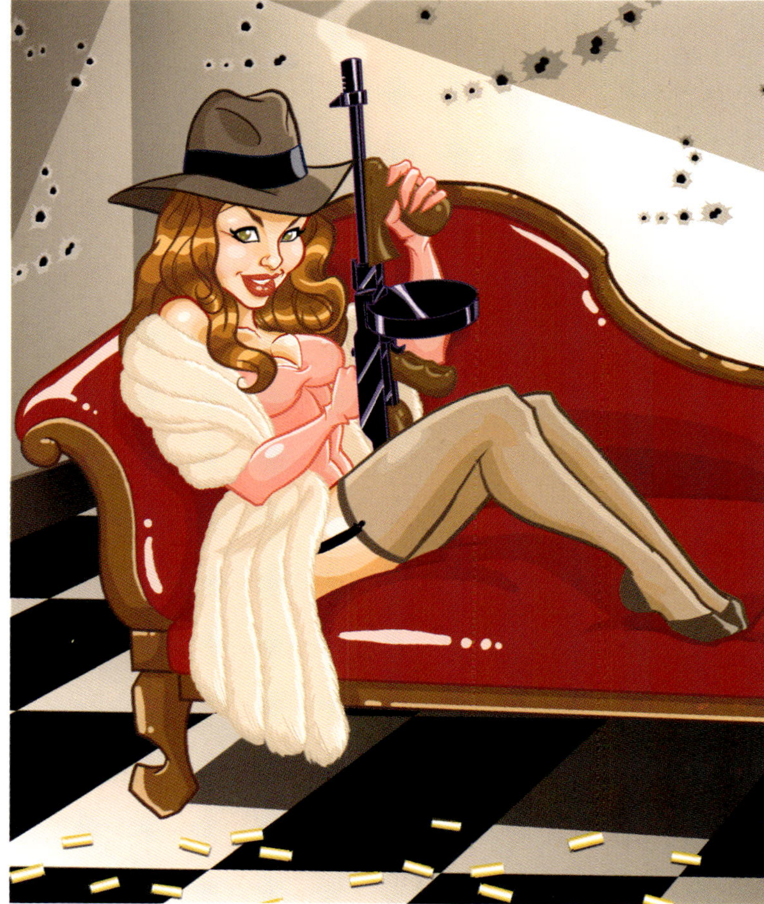

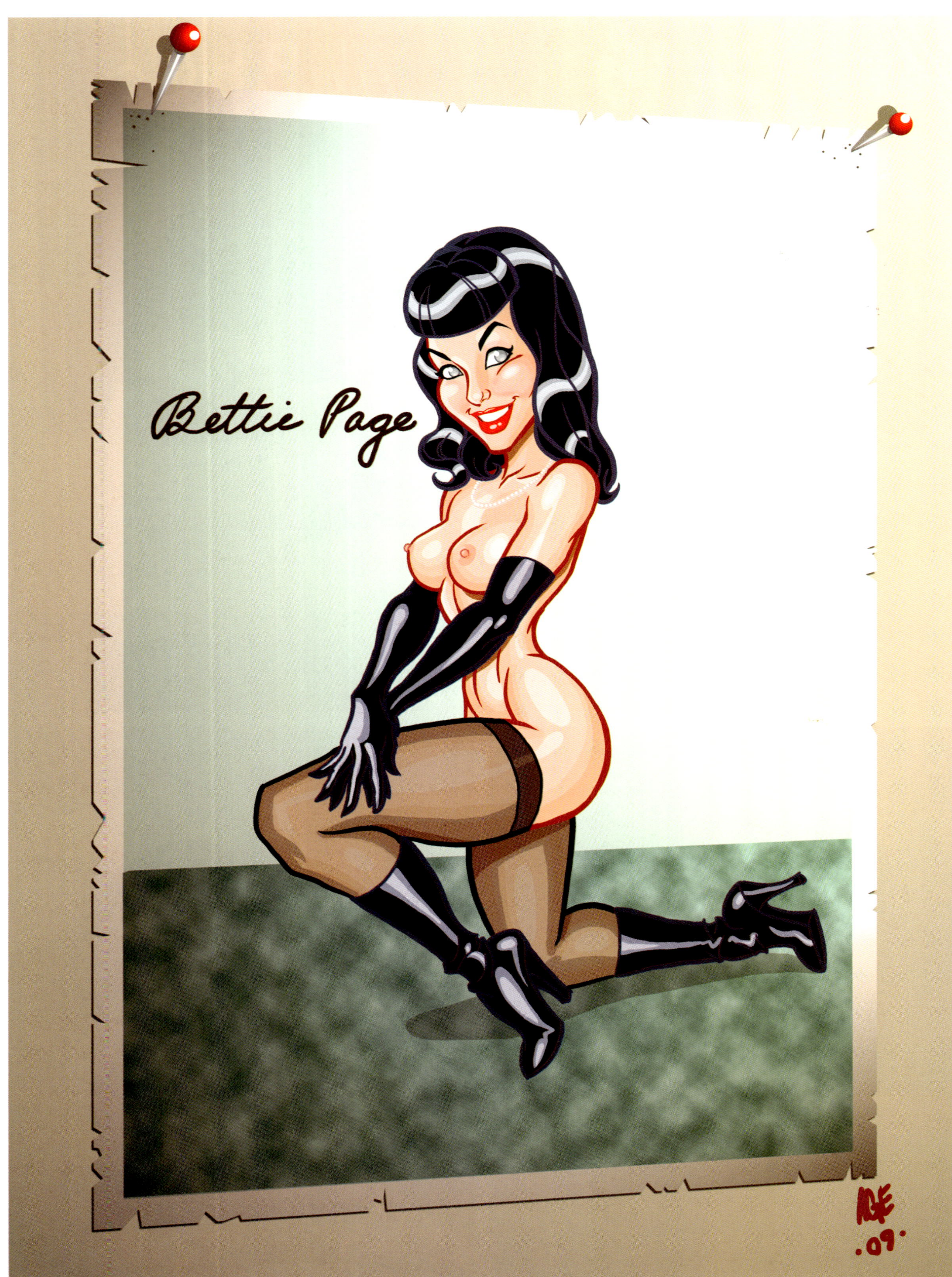
Bettie Page
AGE
.09.

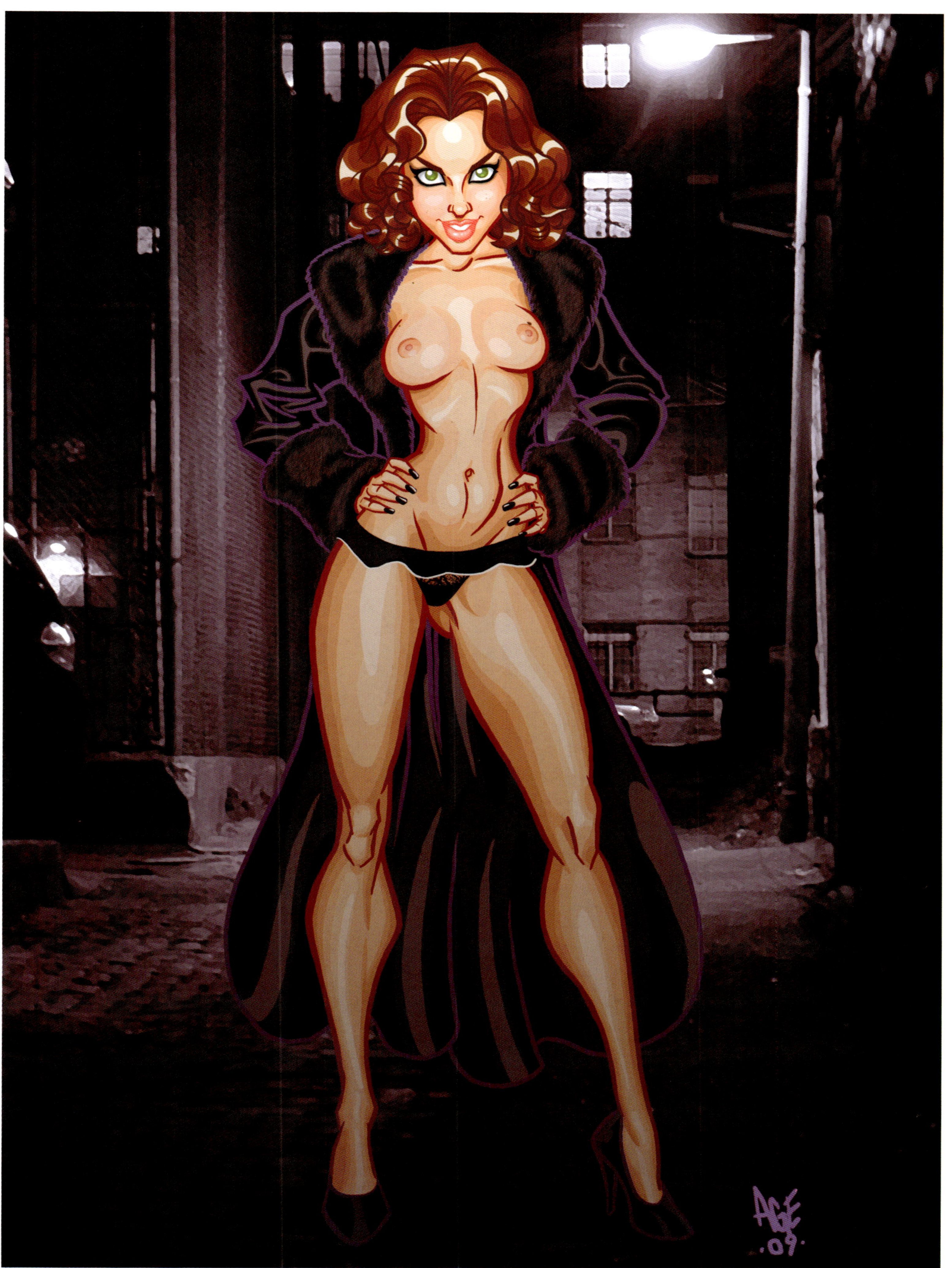

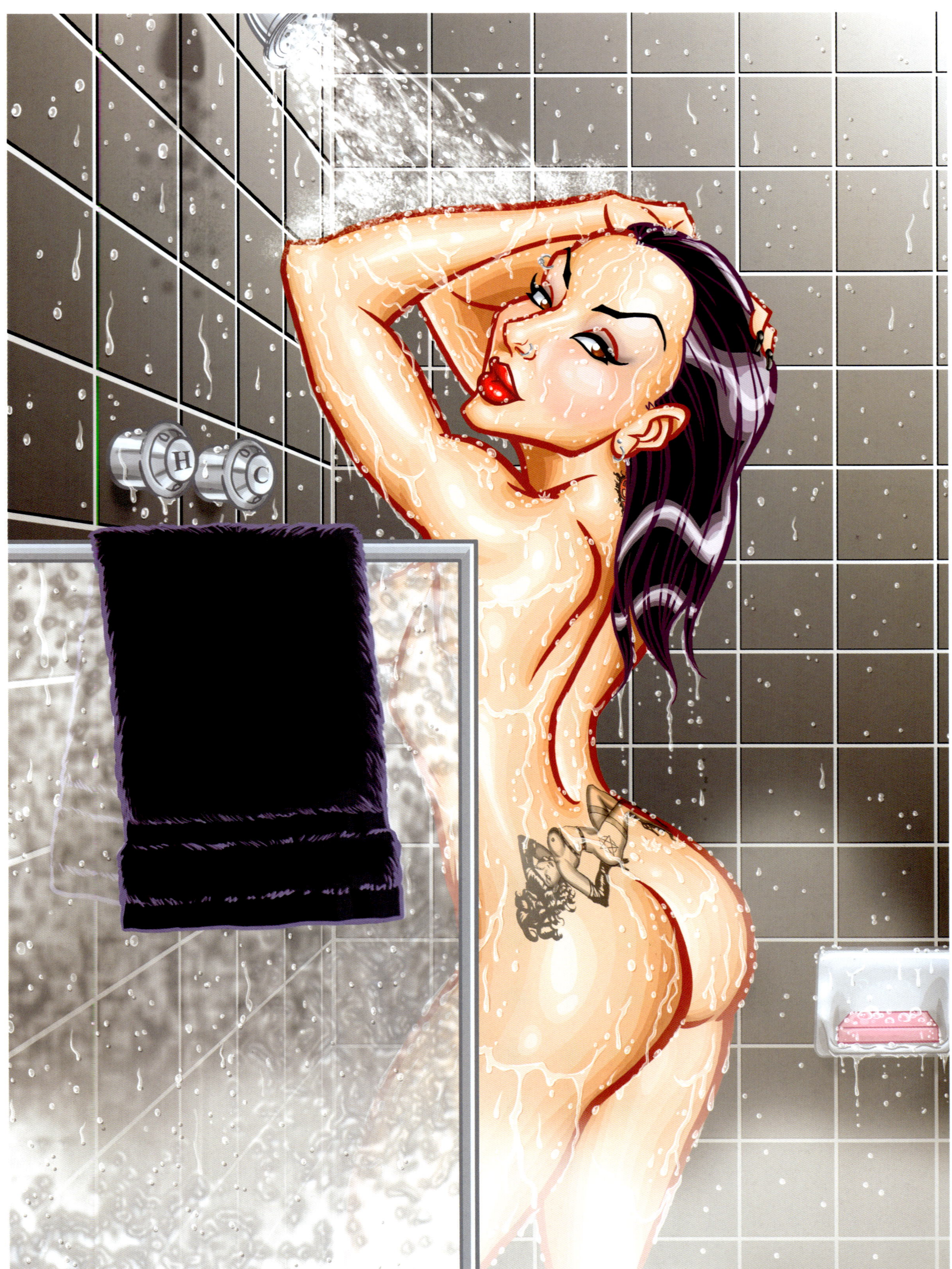
H
C

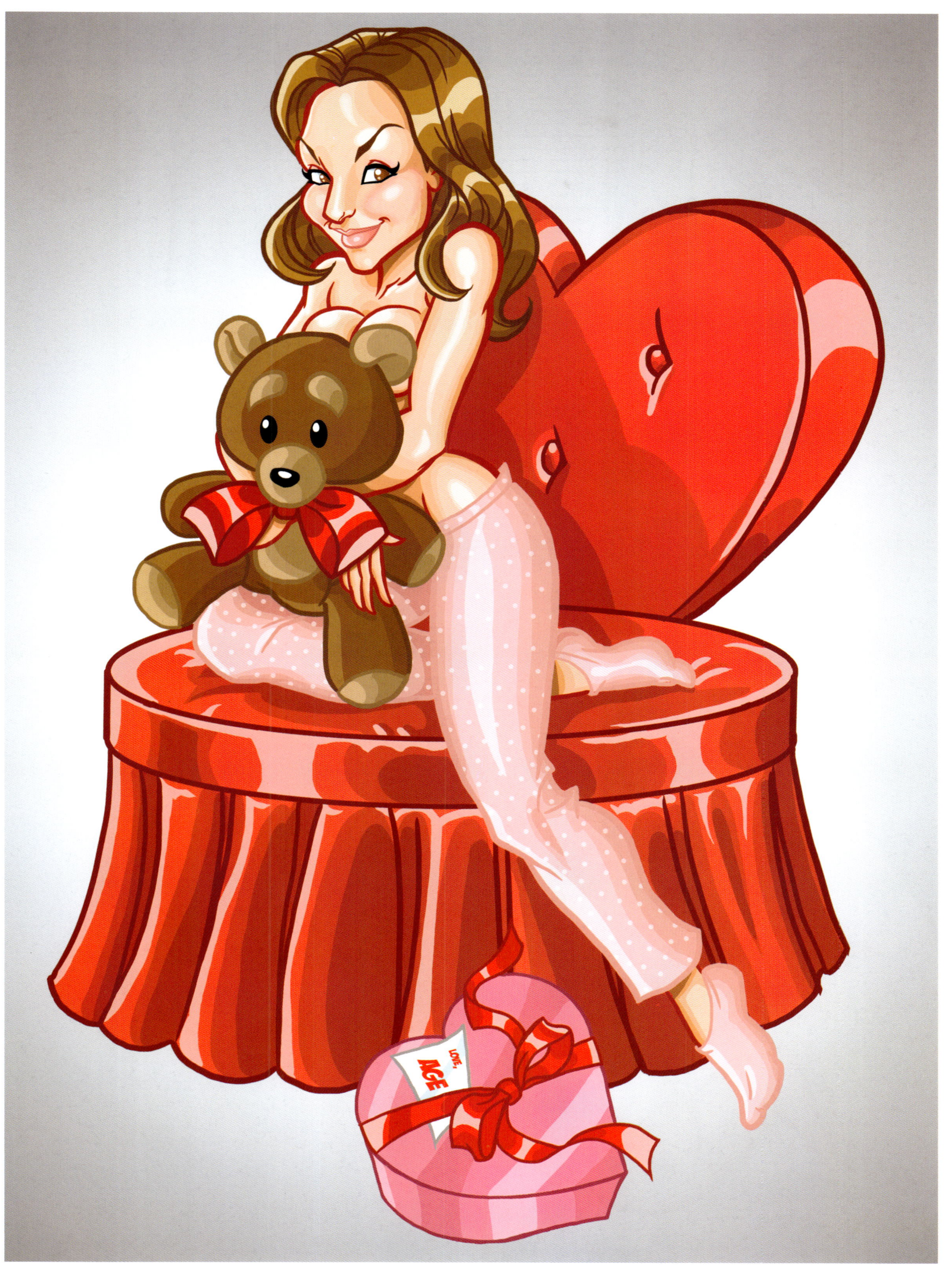
LOVE,
AGE

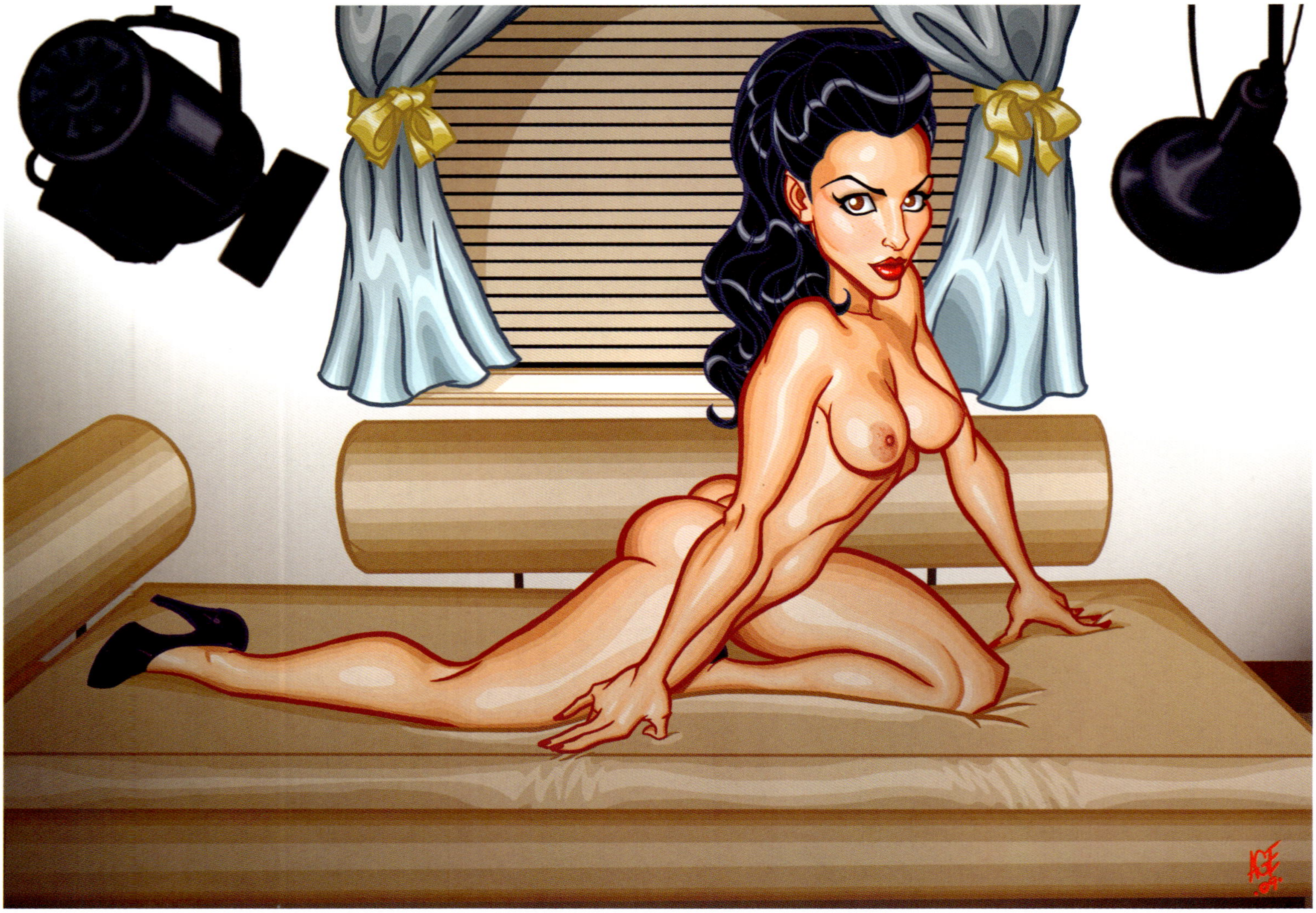

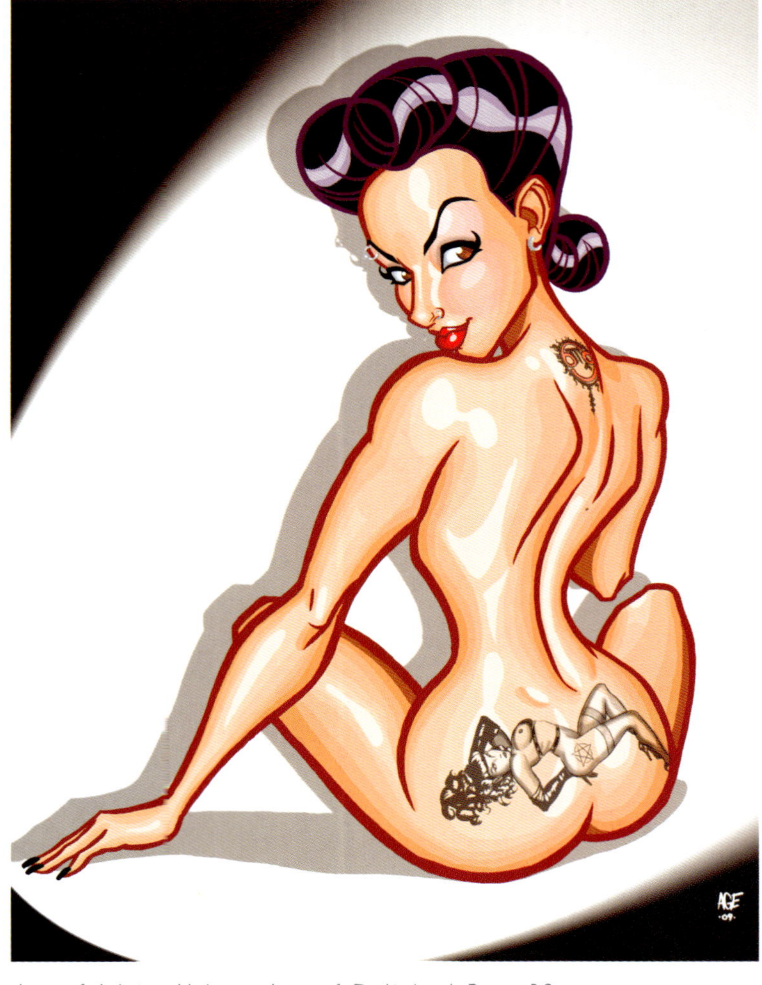

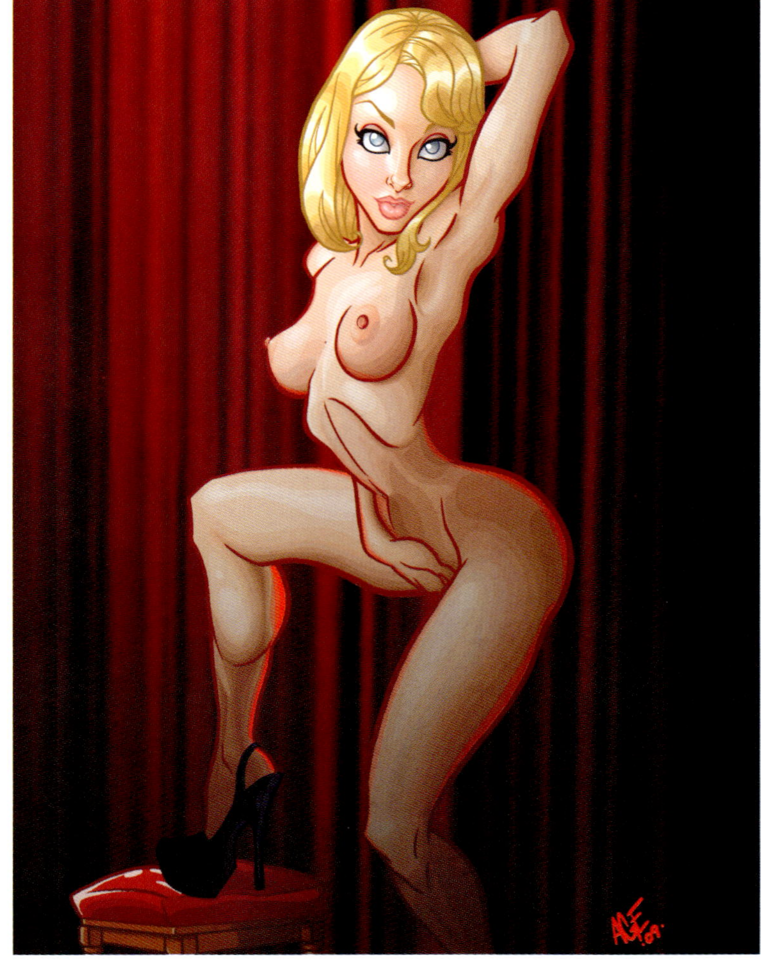

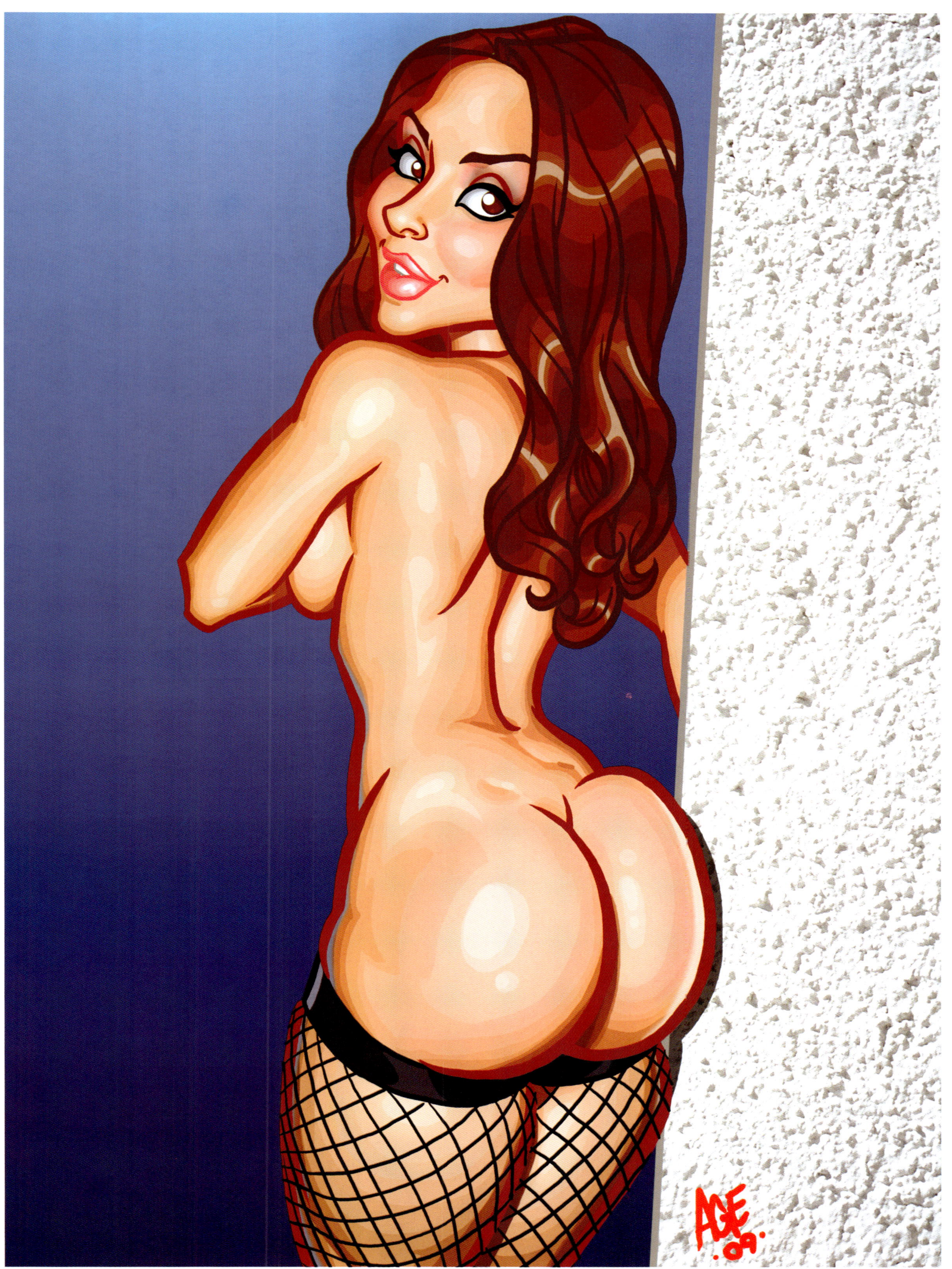
AGE .09.

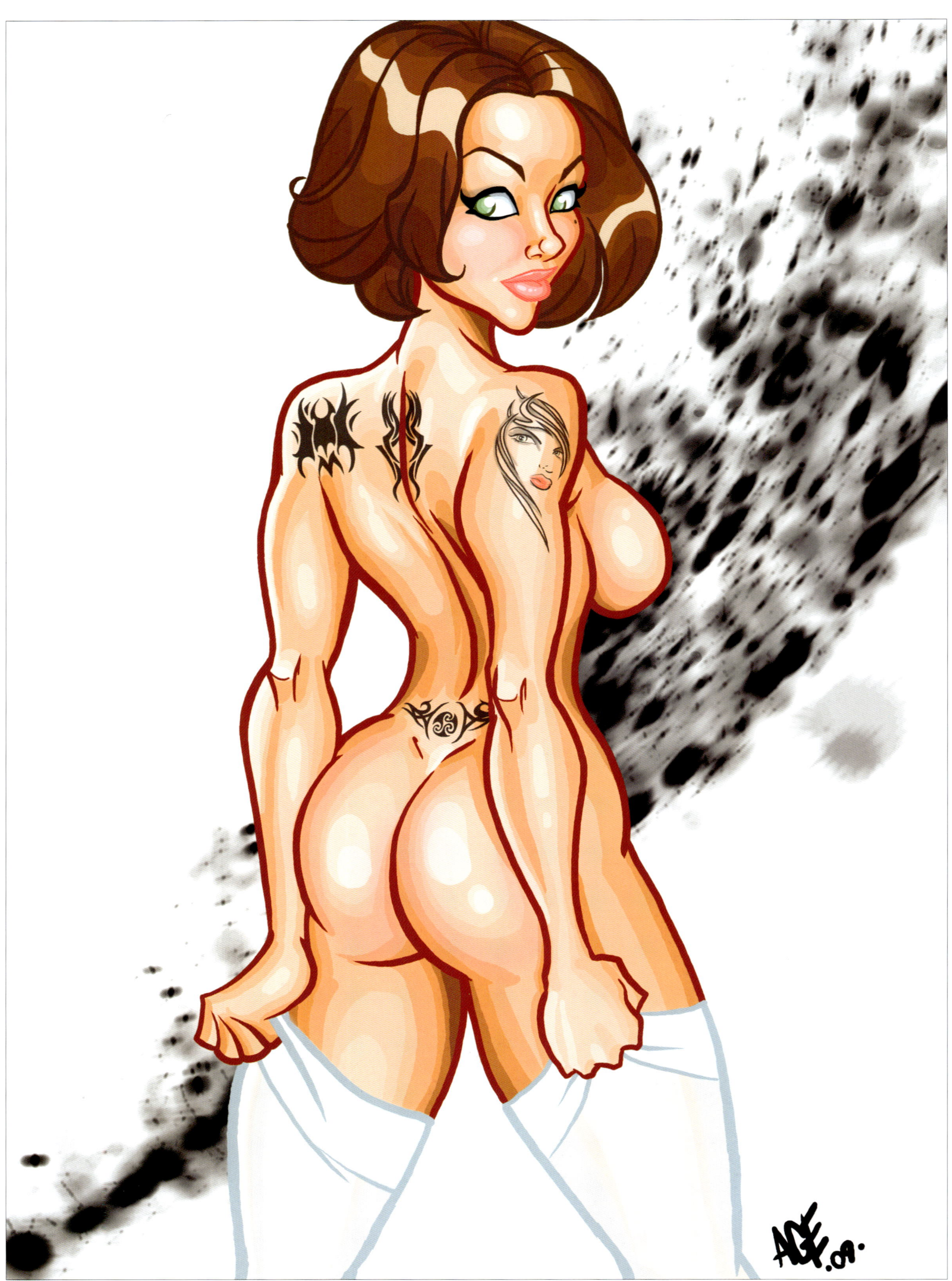

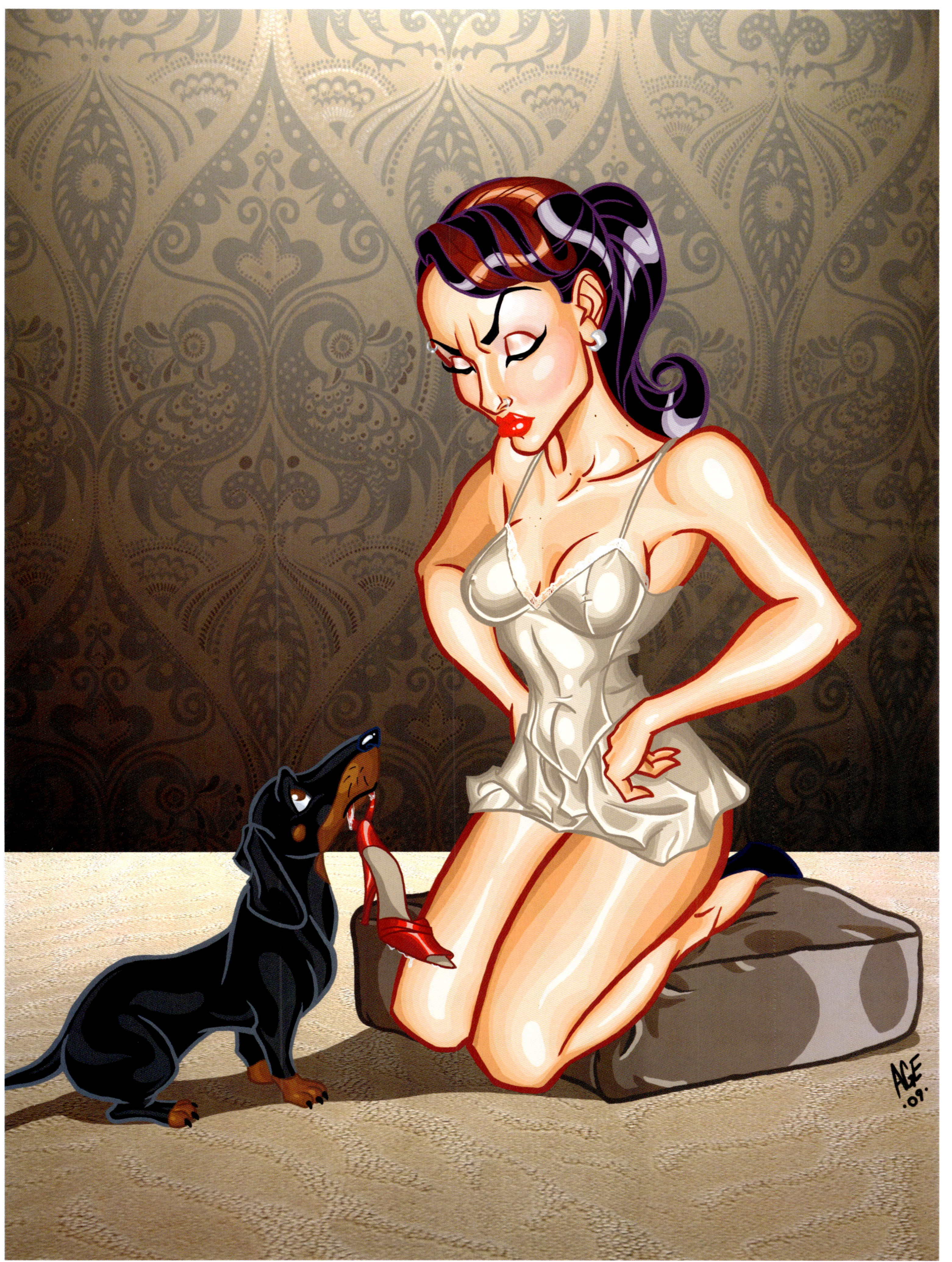

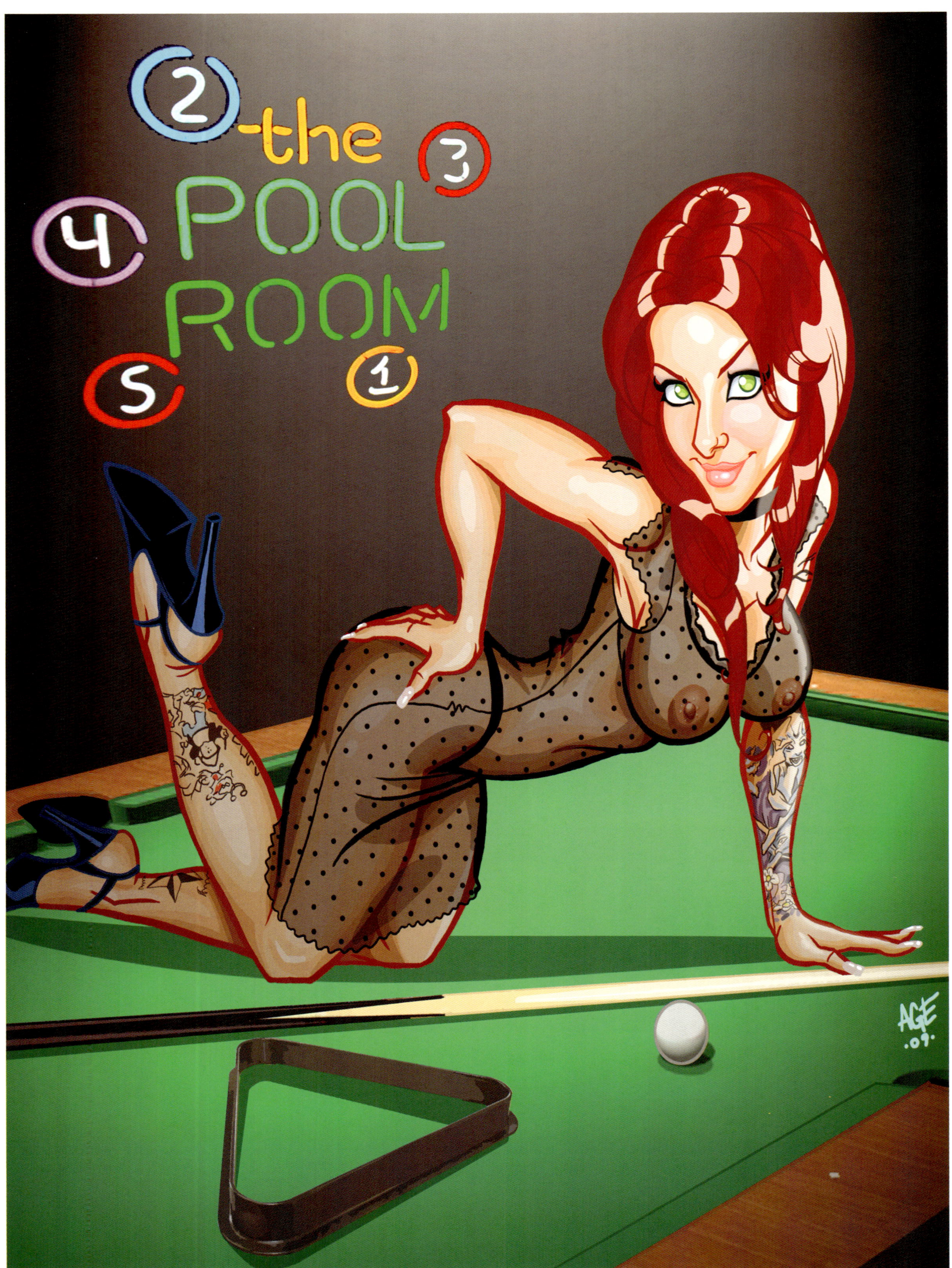
2
-the
3
4
POOL
ROOM
5
1
AGE
.09.

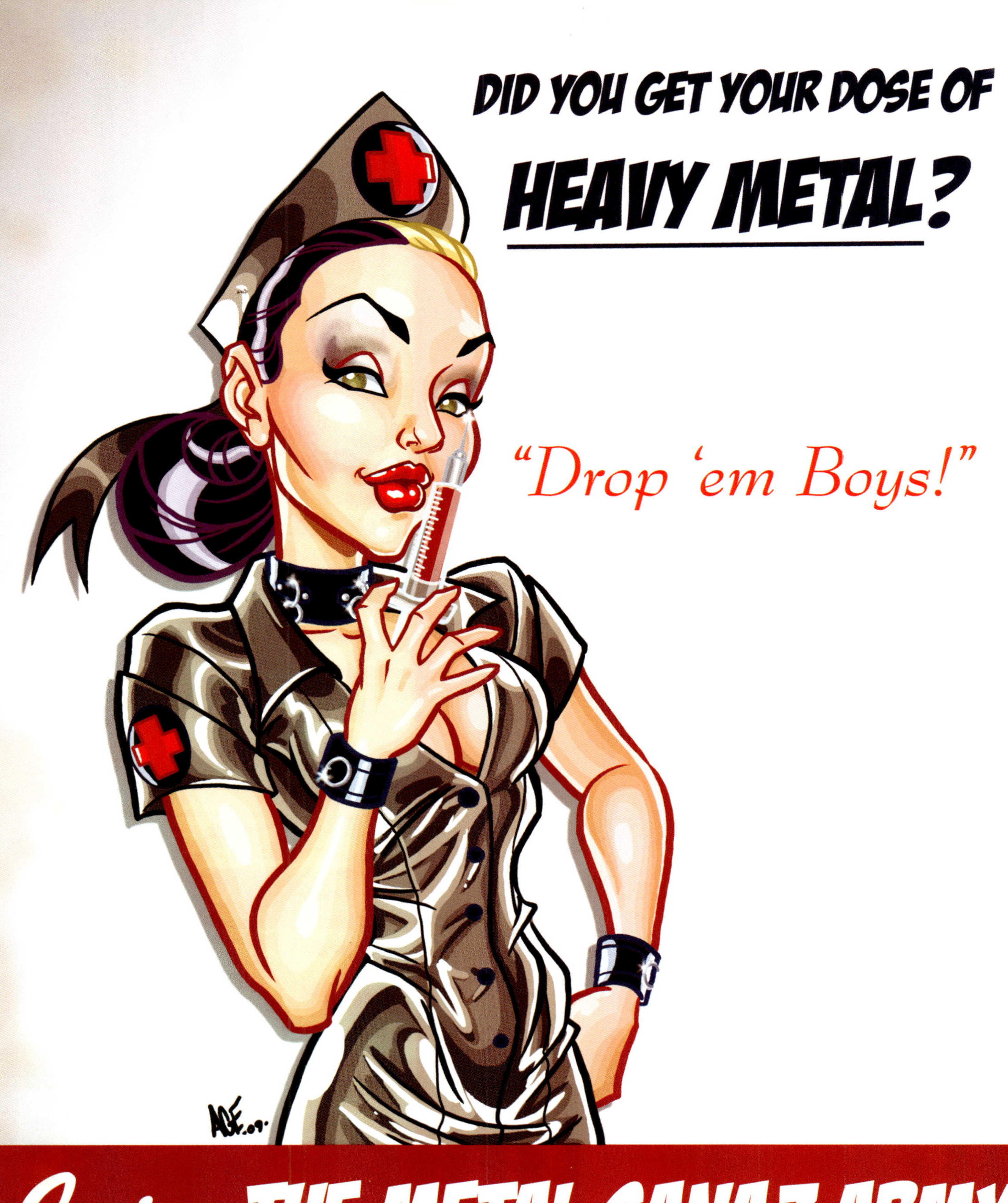
DID YOU GET YOUR DOSE OF
HEAVY METAL?
"Drop 'em Boys!"
Join THE METAL SANAZ ARMY

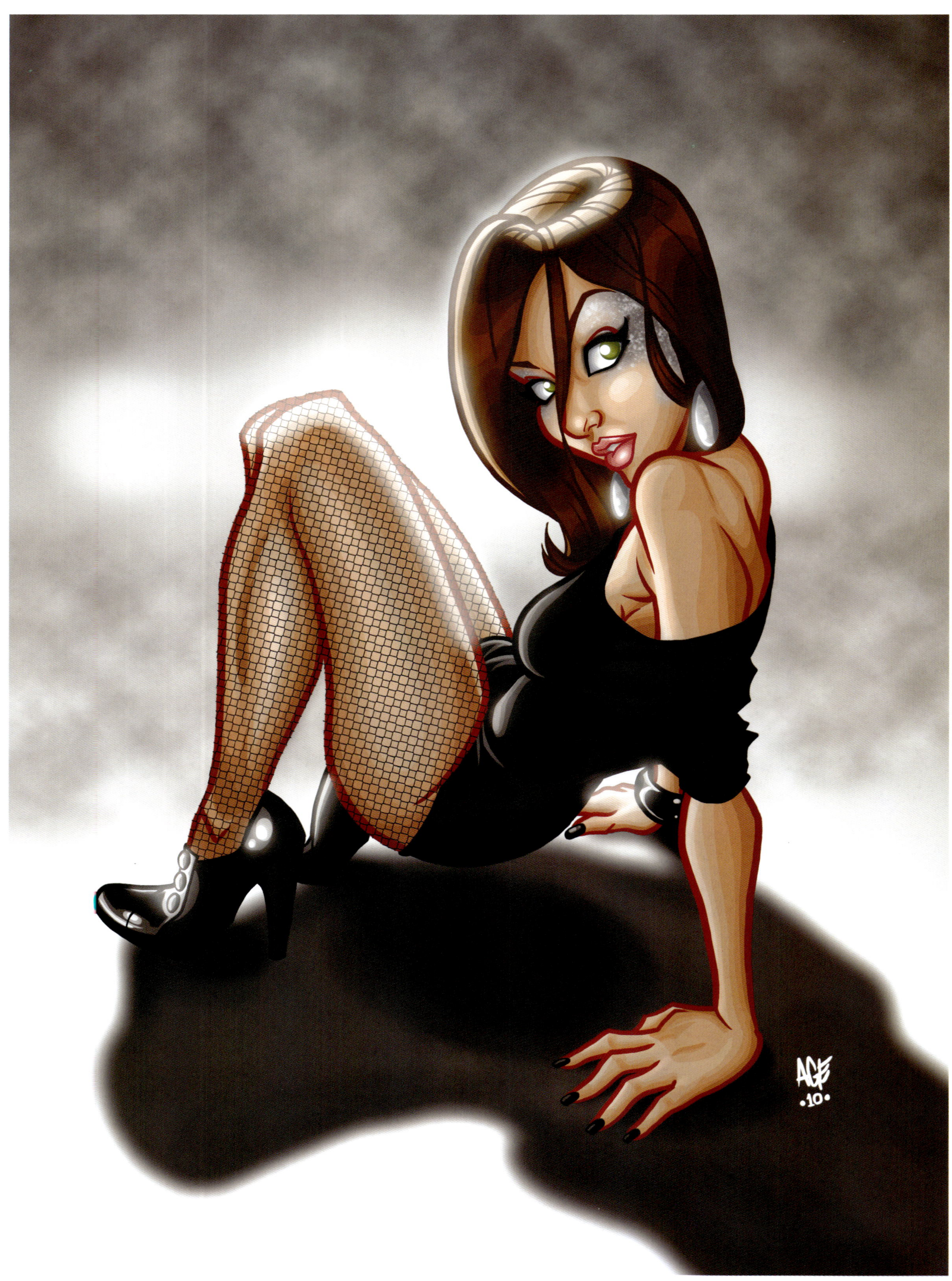
AGE
•10•

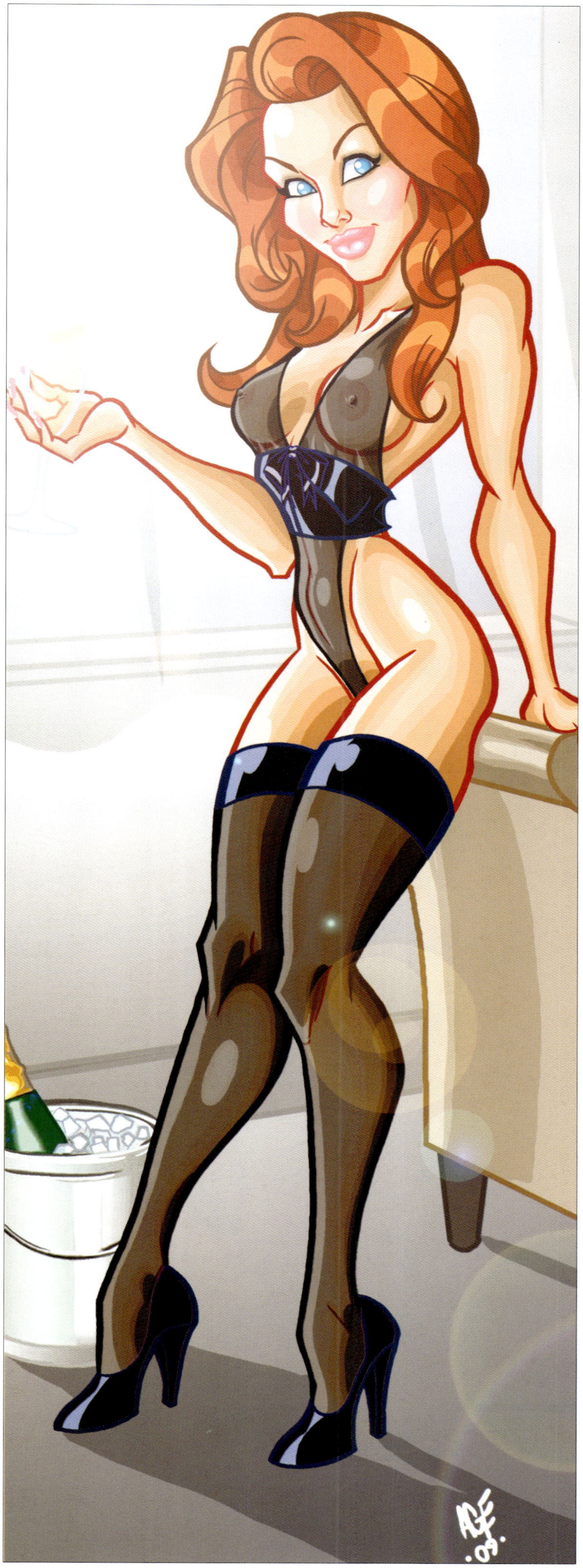

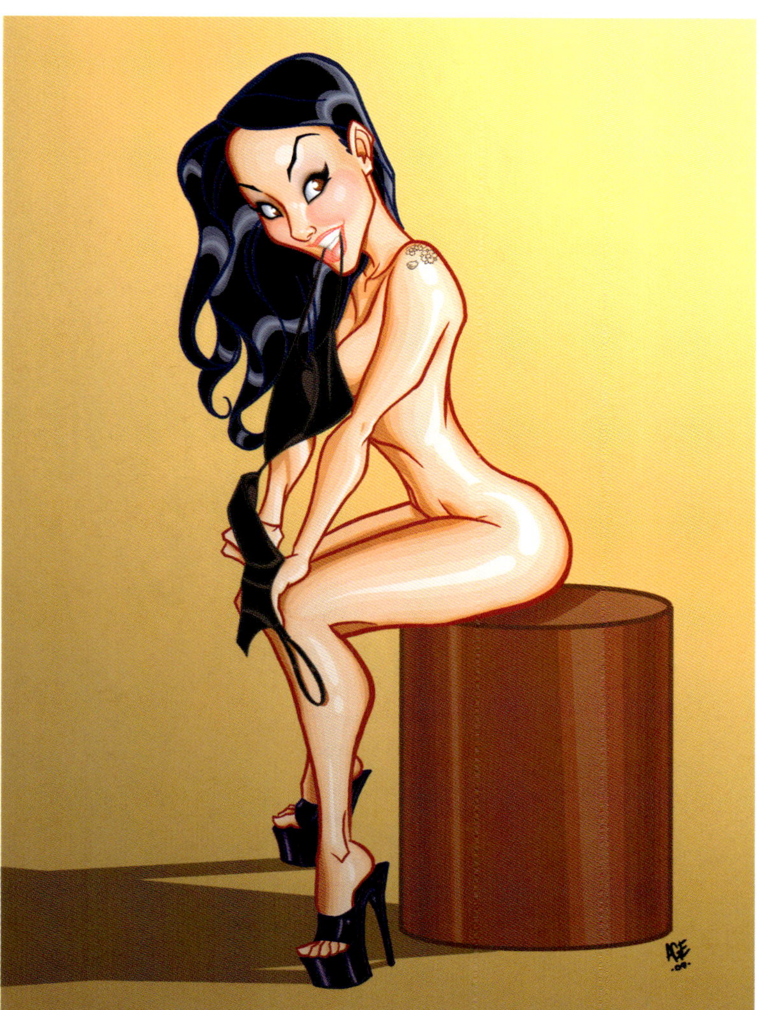

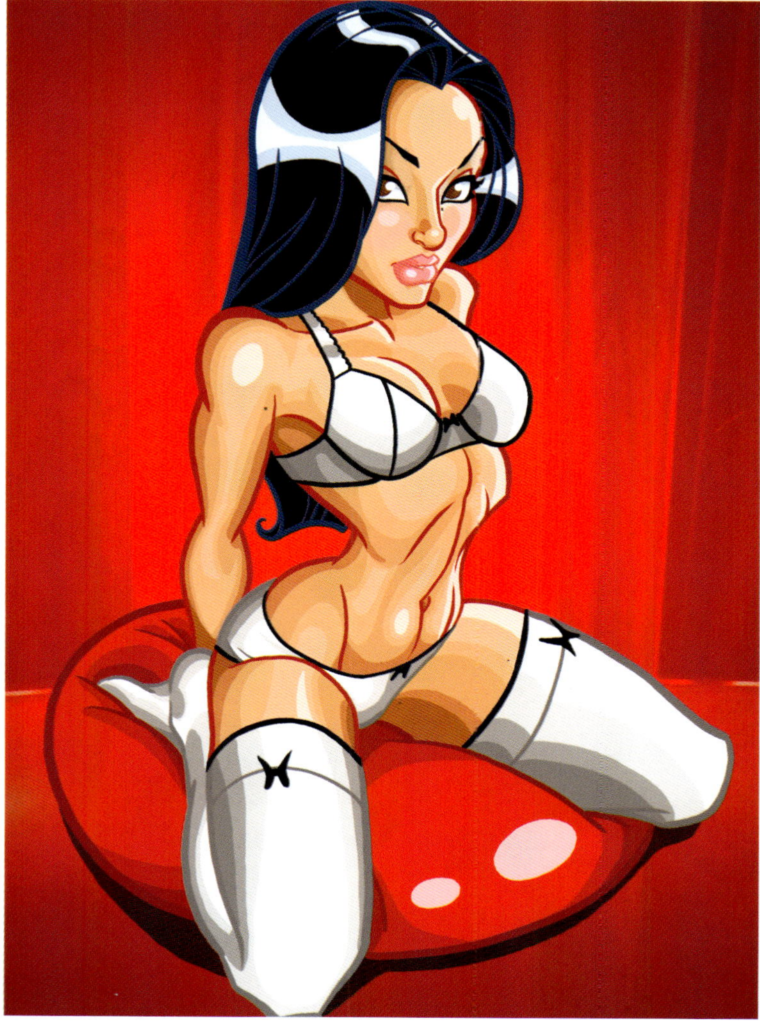

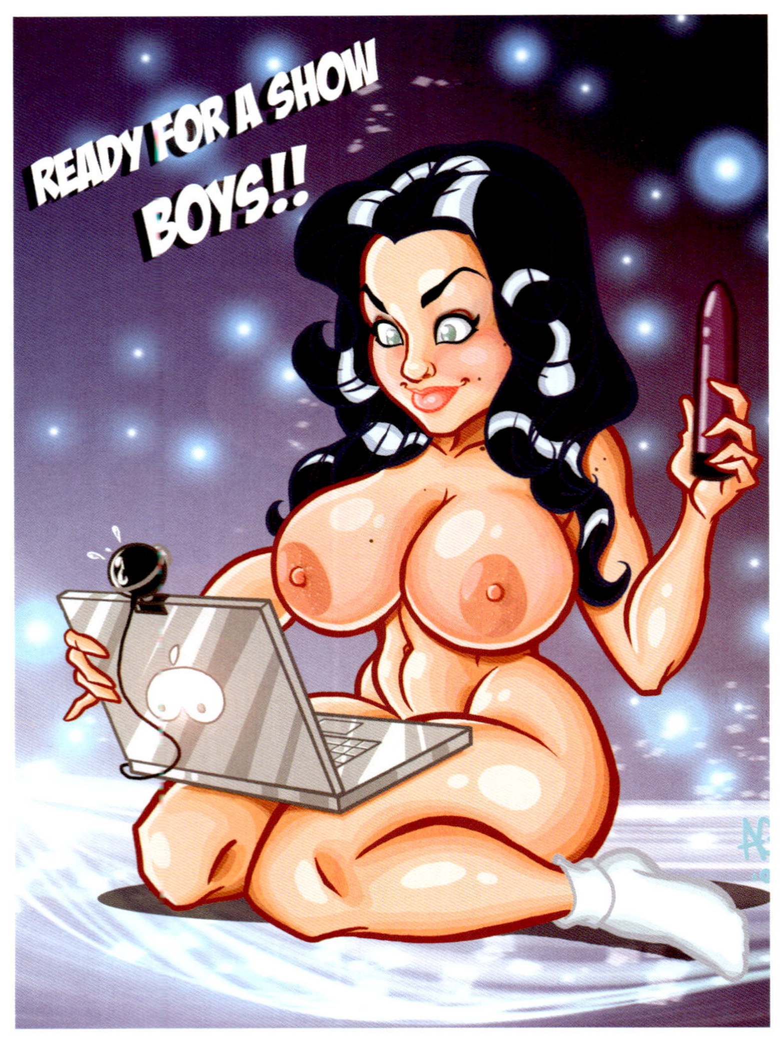
READY FOR A SHOW
BOYS!!

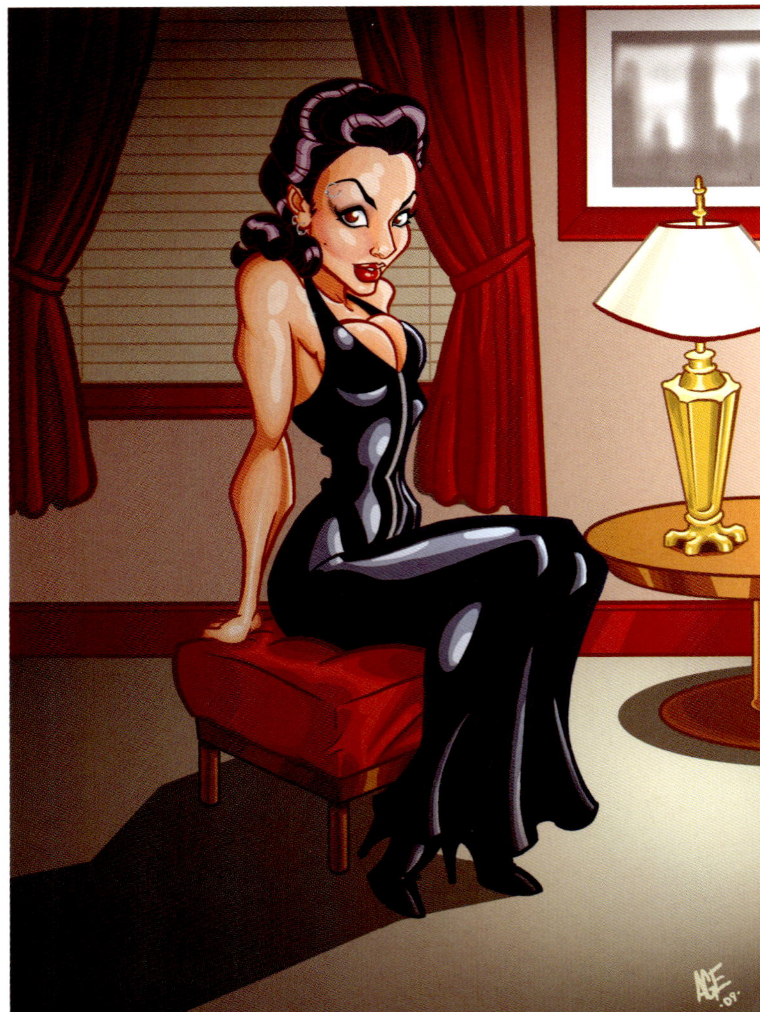

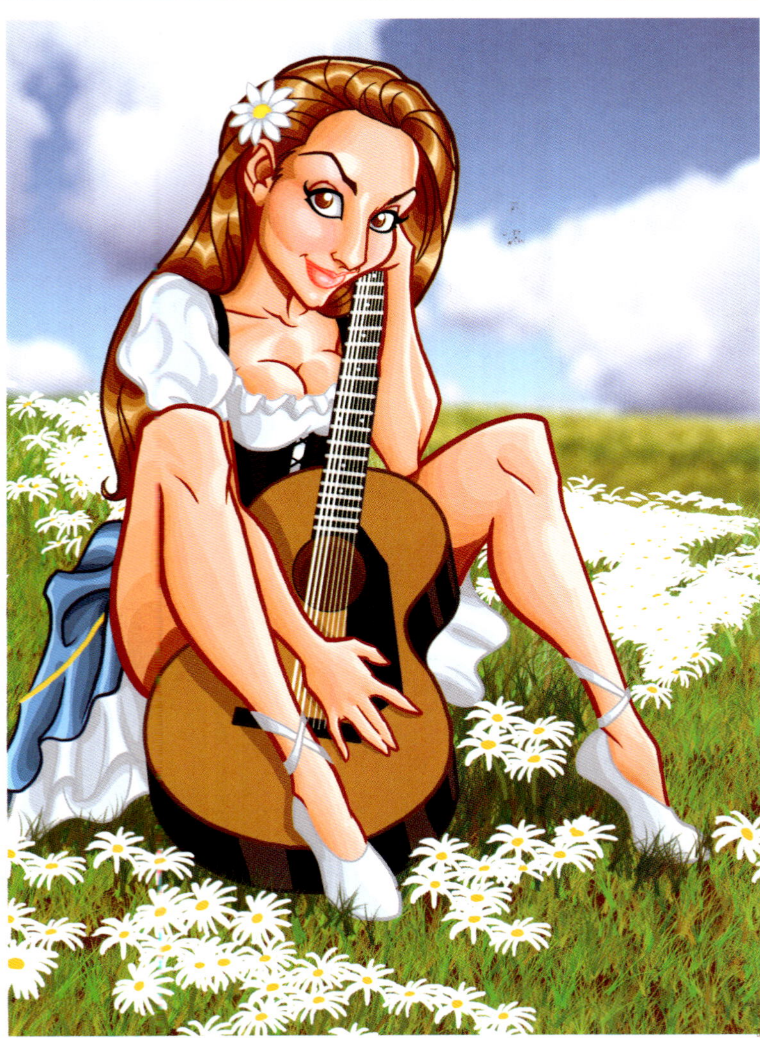

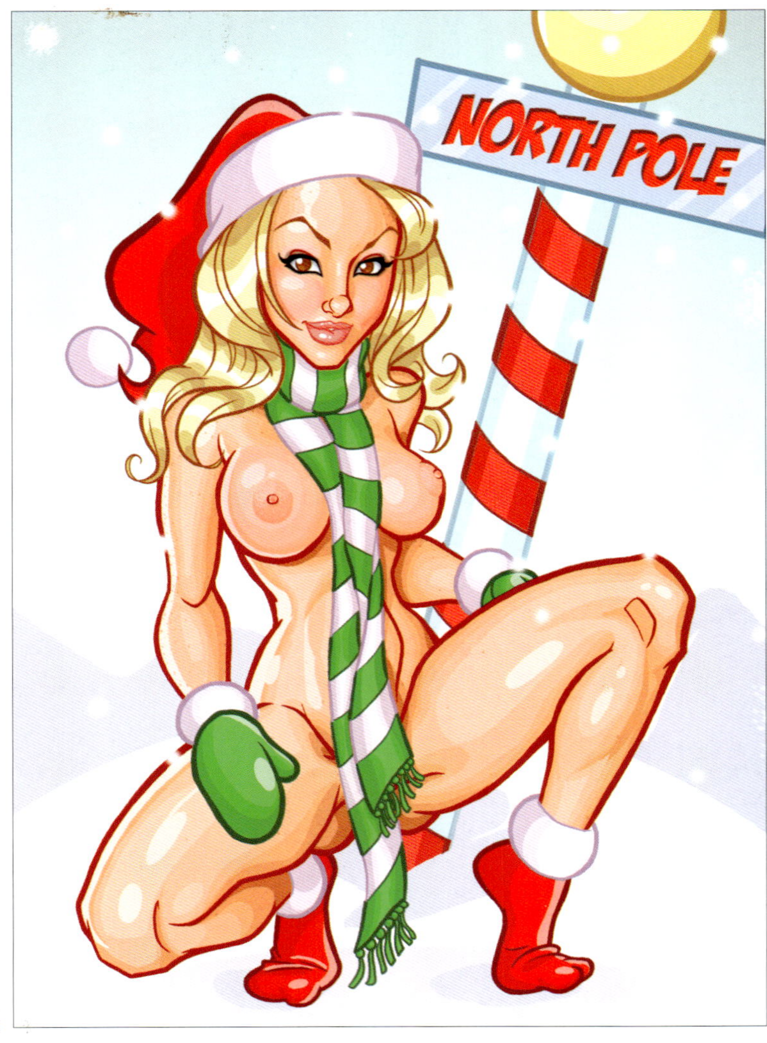
NORTH POLE

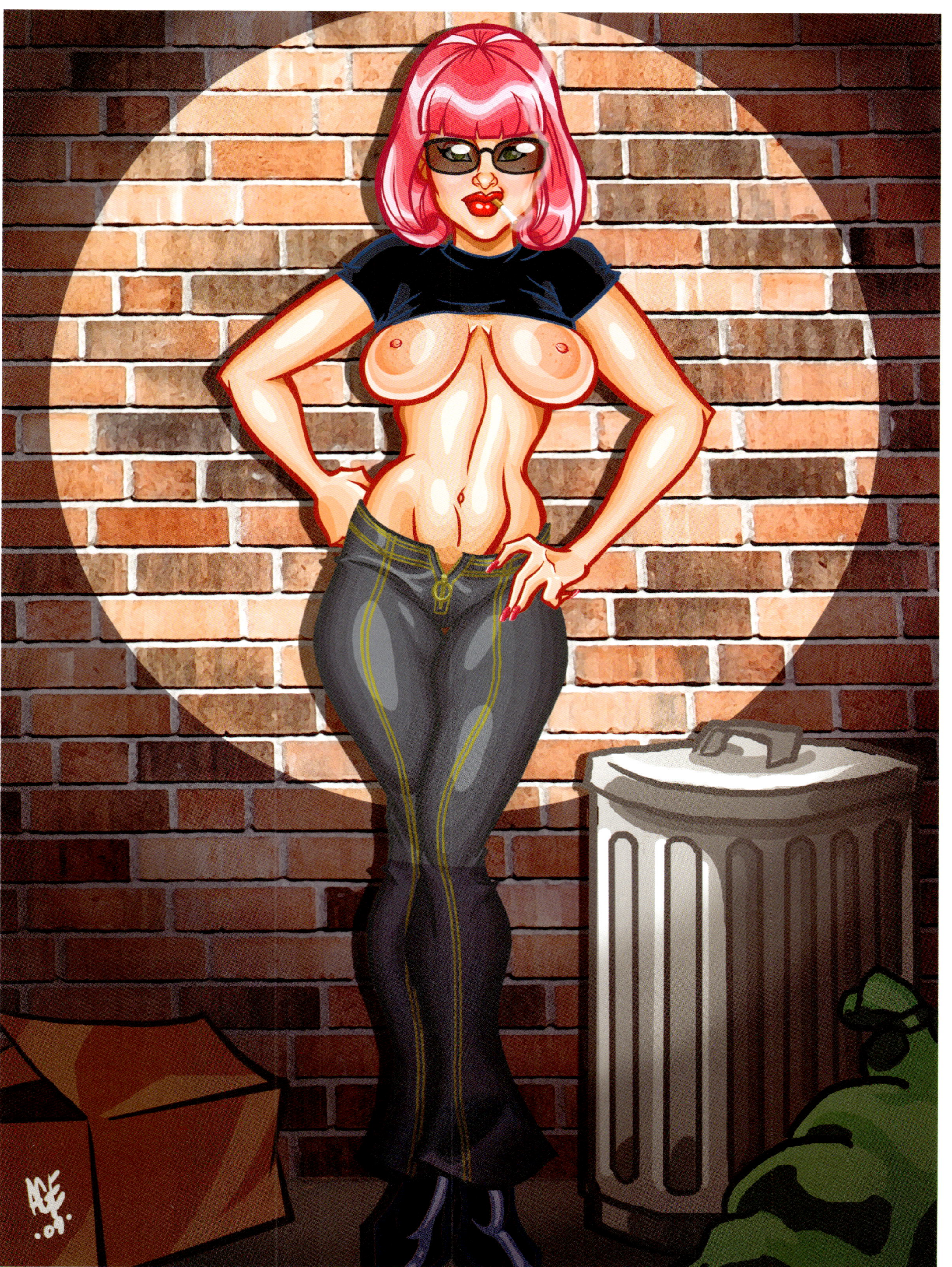

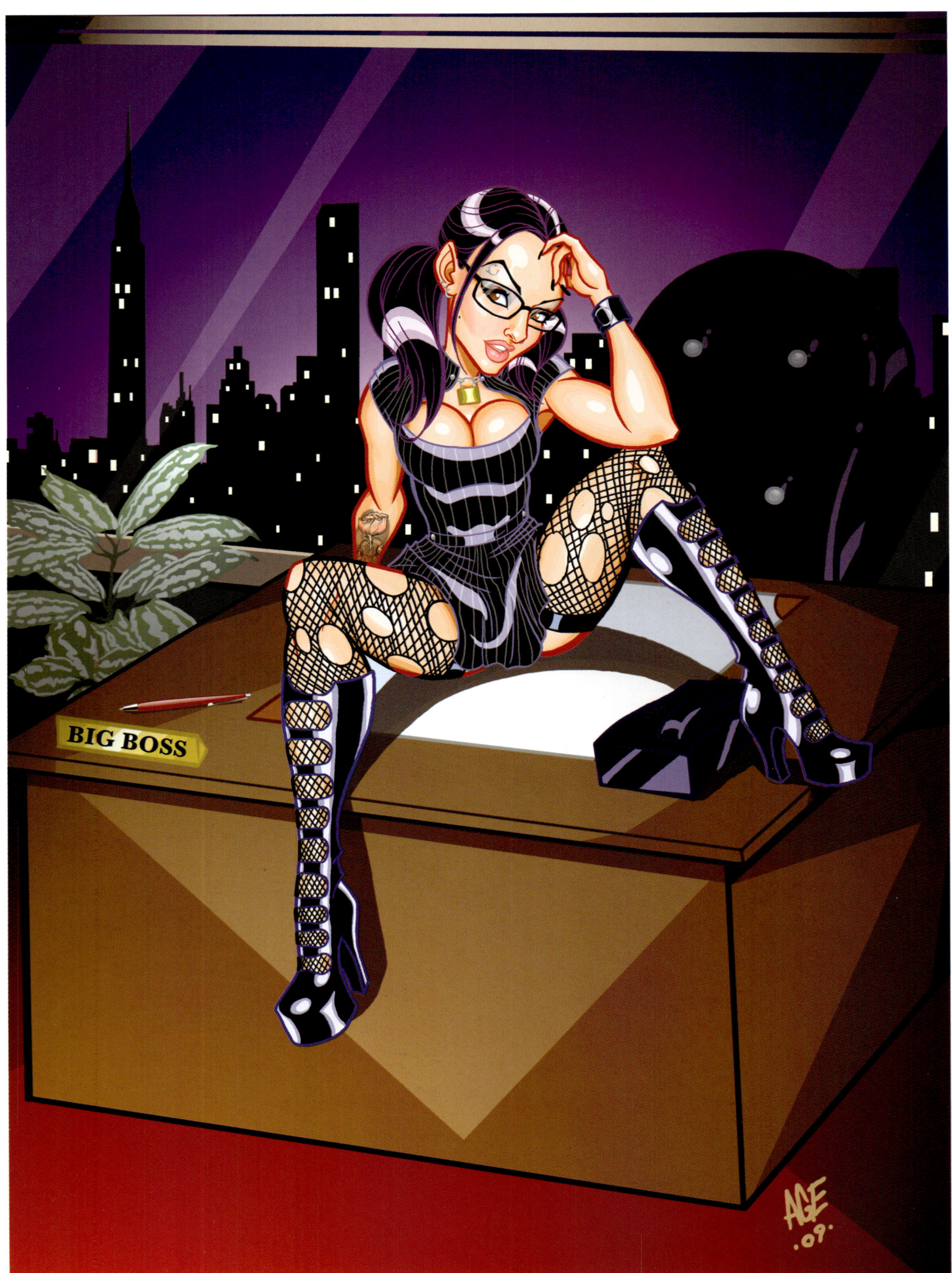
BIG BOSS
AGE
.09.